SUFFERING MAN, LOVING GOD

Also by James Martin

Did Jesus Rise from the Dead?
The Road to the Aisle
A Plain Man in the Holy Land
The Reliability of the Gospels
Letters of Caiaphas to Annas
People in the Jesus Story
William Barclay: A Personal Memoir
Listening to the Bible
My Friend Bobby

JAMES MARTIN is a Church of Scotland minister. He ministered in Newmilns West, Ayrshire for eight years before moving to High Carntyne, Glasgow from which he retired at the end of 1987 after a ministry there of thirty-four years. In addition to his very busy parish work in Glasgow, he was involved with school, hospital, and industrial chaplaincies as well as many church committees. He is well-known for his radio and television work, particularly in Scotland.

A close associate of William Barclay, Dr. Martin revised a number of Professor Barclay's books for new editions, including all seventeen volumes of the famous *Daily Study Bible*.

SUFFERING MAN, LOVING GOD

Reflections and Prayers for Those Who Hurt

James Martin

1817

Harper & Row, Publishers, San Francisco

New York, Grand Rapids, Philadelphia, St. Louis
London, Singapore, Sydney, Tokyo, Toronto

SUFFERING MAN, LOVING GOD: *Reflections and Prayers for Those Who Hurt.*
Copyright © 1990 by James Martin. All rights reserved. Printed in the
United States of America. No part of this book may be used or
reproduced in any manner whatsoever without written permission
except in the case of brief quotations embodied in critical articles and
reviews. For information address Harper & Row, Publishers, Inc., 10
East 53rd Street, New York, NY 10022.

FIRST EDITION

Library of Congress Cataloging-in-Publication Data

Martin, James, 1921-
    Suffering man, loving God : reflections and prayers for those who
hurt / James Martin.—1st ed.
        p. cm.
    ISBN 0-06-065444-9
    1. Suffering—Religious aspects— Christianity.   2. Consolation.
3. Prayers.   I. Title.
BV4909.M37   1990
248.8'6—dc20
                                                              89-45747
                                                                  CIP

90 91 92 93 94 HAD 10 9 8 7 6 5 4 3 2 1

*To my mother, who suffered many things
and suffered them well.
And to my various congregations,
amongst whom I have seen much
suffering and much overcoming of it.*

Contents

Foreword   ix

Introduction   xi

1. Suffering Man   1
2. The Best World Possible?   7
3. "Sent" by God?   14
4. Punishment for Sin?   23
5. Some Further Questions   31
6. Some Alleviating Considerations   45
7. Loving God   53
8. Some Attitudes to the Problem   58
9. The Christian Attitude   66
10. Even in Bereavement   74
11. Twenty Years On   78

Prayers for Suffering People   85

Index   113

Foreword

A book on the problem of suffering is either a book that is completely superficial or a book that does try to get to the heart of the human situation. I have read this book with great interest and with a very great deal of profit because it is one of those books that does try to get to the heart of the situation. No one will ever find a complete solution to the problem of suffering. All that one can really do is to help the sufferer to meet his suffering with faith and courage and I am quite certain that there is no doubt that Mr. Martin has done this. This is a book that will bring comfort, strengthen faith, and provide courage to go on; and it is therefore a very valuable book, valuable out of all proportion to its size. I commend it very highly and I am certain that he who reads it will be able better to face life.

University of Glasgow, WILLIAM BARCLAY
January 1969

Introduction

The problem of human suffering and sorrow is one that mankind has been wrestling with since human time began. My extensive pastoral experience over forty years of ministry has demonstrated to me over and over again, sometimes in heartbreaking fashion, that no problem is more universal and none can be more agonizing.

It was in an attempt to give some help in regard to this problem that this book was written. It tries to deal with it sympathetically because the author, too, has known something of it personally. It tries to give some assistance toward grappling with the mysteries of the various whys and wherefores of suffering. It tries especially, and this is much more important, to give some assistance toward actually combating successfully those experiences of suffering and sorrow, which come to everyone in some form and in some measure some time or other.

My hope and prayer are that it may have some success in these endeavors.

SUFFERING MAN, LOVING GOD

· 1 ·

Suffering Man

THE FACT of human suffering is one that needs no arguing, and fresh evidence of its reality comes to hand every day. Today's newspaper is full of tragic tales, and tomorrow's will contain as many more. Catastrophe and tragedy, sorrow and pain, often on a major scale, are written into the constitution of human life. And they come, as most of us are only too well aware, not only in the large-scale disasters that involve masses of people but also, and sometimes even more poignantly, in the tragedies that intimately affect a single life or a small group of people. Job was expressing the feelings and the findings of all the ages when he said, "Man is born unto trouble, as the sparks fly upward" (Job 5:7).

The fact of human suffering constitutes a real problem for human thought, and particularly for Christian thought. "Why should it be? Why? " Nor is this merely an academic question, a matter for the classroom or the lecture platform or the study, to be lifted and laid as time permits and with complete detachment. On the contrary, this is a question with which everyone sooner or later becomes personally and, it may be, agonizingly concerned. The problem is that of every generation and of everyone in every generation because the experience of suffering is common to all the human race.

Suffering overtakes different people in different ways and afflicts them in different degrees. But it comes, nevertheless, to us all and it is the personal experience of suffering which adds the note of agonized entreaty to the question, "Why?" For with this, as with most things, it is when the matter becomes personalized that it becomes most real.

This is the case, for example, with regard to the suffering of war. War exacts a terrible price in terms of untimely deaths and ruined bodies, shattered homes and broken hearts. We may be keenly aware of this and may share in the pain of it, even though we are not personally involved. But how different it becomes when personal involvement arrives.

I shall always remember a day in early May 1945. All through the war I had felt the burden of its suffering, although at a distance. But on that May morning, with the Victory bells about to join their glad chorus, my widowed mother received a letter from the War Office, terse and businesslike, to say that my brother had been killed in action in Northwest Europe.

Now I knew something of the cost of war in personal terms. Now I knew personally the pain of sudden bereavement. And now the problem of human suffering became all at once more pointed and more urgent.

This is the kind of experience that befalls men and women every single day. Human suffering takes personal form in their own experience and it becomes a problem as never before. And beyond doubt there is a great deal of human suffering in the world. As a random example, let me quote you certain items in a recent working day of mine.

In the morning I conducted the funeral service of a young mother. Twenty-five years old, she left three children under school age. Her husband, on Merchant Navy service, had been on a Far East trip and had not seen his wife for over a year. When news of her sudden and serious illness reached him he flew home at once from Hong Kong—but she died the day before he reached her.

In the afternoon I visited some sick people and I mention three particularly. One was a young woman in a maternity hospital. It was her first baby but it had lived only a few minutes. Another was a woman, with two teenage children, who was dying slowly and painfully of cancer. The third was an older woman, so severely crippled by arthritis that the future held no promise except the hospital bed in which she lay in constant pain.

My evening included a call from a man who wanted to share with me the shattering news that his wife, in her thirties and with three school-age children, had an inoperable cancer and must soon die.

These items did not belong to an extraordinary day. They were part of a fairly ordinary day, a day which just because it was not unusual underlines Job's declaration that man is born to trouble.

The fact of human suffering is both real and universal and so is the problem which it presents. "Why is there such a thing as suffering? Why should this happen to me?"

In its most acute form, the problem of human suffering is a problem of Christian faith. It is when we believe that God is made known in Jesus Christ that the fact that men and women suffer so much assumes its most bewildering perplexity. If God is love, as Jesus reveals, should not suffering be impossible? But suffering does occur. How, then, is it to be reconciled with our belief in the love of God?

In the classical statement of the problem it is affirmed that God cannot be both loving and omnipotent. If He were, obviously He would not allow suffering to occur.

Since, however, it does, God must either be loving but not omnipotent, or omnipotent but not loving. Suffering is a fact; therefore God either does not care or is powerless to prevent it.

So runs the argument in its classical form. But the Christian cannot accept its conclusions.

The Christian begins from the conviction that God is both love and omnipotence. A minister may well begin a prayer in public worship with, "Almighty God, our loving heavenly Father." The phrase is a recognition of God's power and God's love. The Christian believes that Jesus has revealed God and that He has shown Him to possess these attributes.

It is when this belief is set alongside the undeniable fact of human suffering that the Christian finds himself up against it, or so it would seem. How may we take account of suffering and still maintain that God is both all-powerful and all-loving? It is here that the problem comes into sharpest focus.

Robert Browning states it like this in the poem Mihrab Shah:

> Wherefore should any evil hap to man—
> From ache of flesh to agony of soul—
> Since God's All-mercy makes All-potency?
> Nay, why permits He evil to Himself—
> Man's sin accounted such? Suppose a world
> Purged of all pain, with fit inhabitant—
> Man pure of evil in thought, word and deed—
> Were it not well? Then, wherefore otherwise?

Wherefore? Why? In every age the cry goes up, often—painfully—from the rack of actual experience. In our day it is uttered by a host of voices, perhaps with even greater urgency and deeper anguish than ever before.

This book will try to listen to that cry and give some answer to it.

That is not its sole purpose, nor even its chief purpose. The problem of human suffering is not only the problem of this eternal "Why?" The problem runs on to that other question, even more important, "How?" How are we to face up? How may we win through?

Even if the Why? of human suffering could be answered with complete satisfaction, we should still have the *fact* of suffering with which to contend. The How? of suffering is the major part of its problem and with it, too, this book will try to deal.

The problem of suffering is with us all. Some try to run away from it or to pretend that it does not exist.

I have an (imaginary) little friend named Bobby of whom I speak to the children in my congregation. One day Bobby paid a visit to the carnival with his parents and his young sister, Susan. In the course of the visit the children took a trip on the Ghost Train, which is a shuddery little journey with various spine-chilling objects coming at you suddenly out of the darkness.

When the trip was completed and all the frightening encounters left behind, Bobby said to Susan, "Were you frightened?"

To his surprise his sister replied, "No, I was not frightened."

"What?" he cried. "Were you really not frightened by the skeletons and the ghosts and the other things?"

"No," insisted Susan, "I wasn't. I didn't see them. I kept my eyes shut all the time."

There are some who adopt precisely this attitude to the problem of human suffering. But it is a foolish attitude, for sooner or later the problem will become so personal that it can no longer be ignored.

Let me finish my story of Bobby and the Ghost Train. When he had completed his interrogation of Susan, she retaliated by asking if he had been frightened.

"Yes," admitted Bobby, rather astonishingly, "I *was* frightened—but I was holding Dad's hand, so it was all right."

Later in this book I will be suggesting that, no matter what suffering may befall us, if we have hold of our Father's hand it will be "all right."

That is when we come on to the "How?" part of the problem. First we must try to deal with the "Why?" and as seriously and as honestly as we are able.

If God is love and God is all-powerful, why should there be suffering?

We must try to offer some answer to this question, for it deeply troubles many minds and may disturb or even shatter faith. "Probably more people lose faith in God through what seems to them the maladjustment of Providence than through any other cause."[1]

Every minister has met something of this. How often he hears someone say, "I can't understand why this thing should have been allowed to happen," or "I prayed and prayed for her recovery but she died," or "He was a good man and did not deserve to have such pain," or "It's a thing like this that puts a strain on one's faith."

The "Why?" of suffering is an inescapable question: and we try to give some answer to it by looking at a few related questions.

NOTES

1. H. Wheeler Robinson, *Suffering, Human and Divine,* p. 45.

· 2 ·

The Best World Possible?

ON ONE HAND stands the Christian belief in the love and the omnipotence of God. On the other the very obvious fact of human suffering. Together these two things pose the question, "Could not God have made the world a better place than it is?"

Many feel strongly that God could and should. They re-echo the sentiments of Omar Khayyám when he said that he would like:

> To grasp this sorry scheme of things entire
> . . . Shatter it to bits, and then
> Remold it nearer to the heart's desire.

This, however, is not the view of Christian faith. Knowing God as He is revealed in Jesus Christ, the Christian is convinced that the world which God has created must be the best world possible. How his conviction is to be reconciled with the incidence of suffering is the concern of this chapter.

On the face of it, such an attempt at reconciliation may appear a hopeless endeavor. For it has to contend with several formidable difficulties. There is, for one, the fact that there is suffering at all. Added to this is the fact that there is so much. Then there is the fact that suffering often affects the innocent. It is not surprising that even Christians are sometimes led to ask whether, after all, this is a bad world rather than a good one; or to wonder, at least, why God did not create something a great deal better than the world as it is.

For the sake of having the picture complete, it must be said that there is another side to the world besides its pain and its shadow and its ugliness. There is, too, much that is lovely and bright and glad. In any judgment of whether God has made a good or bad world, this must be taken into account.

Most people find life a desirable thing, something that they enjoy and are reluctant to let go:

> Can any of you deny that it is a universe worth living in? Any such denial would be drowned in the gigantic chorus of the infinite millions who have lived and who have loved life. Why, the whole of literature is pierced with the cry of the shortness of life and the misery of death. We have so much enjoyed the days which have been given to us by God that it is with bitter regret that we bid them goodbye—even when religion has put before us the prospect of an immortal life of much greater happiness.[1]

It is true, of course, that some have been engulfed in the world's pain and tasted little of its joy. And some have found the world so unhappy a place that they have destroyed their own lives to escape from it. But these are a small minority. The vast majority have found life good, despite its pain, and, like George Borrow's *Lavengro*, have judged it sweet.

> "Life is sweet, brother!"
> "Do you think so?"
> "Think so? There's night and day, brother, both sweet things; sun, moon and stars, brother, all sweet things: there's likewise a wind on the heath. Life is very sweet, brother."
> "What if you're sick, Jaspar?"
> "There's the sun and the stars, brother."

"What if you're blind, Jaspar?"
"There's the wind on the heath, brother"

This is something that it is well to keep in mind. But what is far more important, when we are considering whether or not to count this a good world, is the standard of judgment we employ. So often we make human happiness the sole criterion. But *is* it the sole criterion? Is it even the chief criterion?

If this were the only, or the most important, criterion, it would scarcely be possible to escape the conclusion that our world was certainly not the best possible world and that in its making God had slipped up badly. But "best possible world" does not necessarily mean "best" in terms of human pleasure or painlessness. It means "best" in terms of God's loving purposes. The Christian believes that these purposes are not concerned primarily with man's immediate happiness (although not indifferent to that) but rather with his ultimate happiness, the development of his personality and the fashioning of a soul fit for eternity. And he believes that this world is the best God could possibly have created for the achievement of these purposes, a world where the possibility of pain and suffering must exist.

In face of this it may still be argued that God might have made a better job of things. It may be contended that He could surely have arranged it so that the amount of suffering in the world was greatly reduced, if not eliminated altogether.

Is there cogency in such an argument? The only way in which this end could be obtained would involve a complete rearranging of the world as it is, and any such rearranging would make it, would it not, a worse not a better world.

Human suffering comes as the result of the processes of natural law or of human choice or, most often, of a combination of the two. It seems to me that both these factors are essential to that "best possible world" which will make for the fashioning of personalities fit for eternal fellowship with God.

Natural law is essential. If we are to grow as moral personalities we must grow in a world which is orderly and reliable. If we were set in a world not ruled by law, in which everything was chaos and anarchy, moral progress would become impossible—not to speak of material progress and of material happiness. We need only think what it would be like if the physical laws of our world were suddenly suspended:

> It needs little reflection to see that *order* is the *sine qua non* of a moral world ... if we never knew within reasonable limits what was going to happen next; if water might suddenly freeze in mid-summer; if the specific gravity of lead might at any time become that of thistledown; if pigs might fly or the Houses of Parliament turn into green cheese—man's life would be a nightmare, not merely because it would be unpleasant but because it could have no moral meaning.[2]

Human freedom also is essential for this to be the "best world possible." Unless man has the power to make his own choices, even if they should be the wrong choices, he is reduced to a mere puppet. If God were to compel men always to choose what is good and wise this would, it is true, greatly reduce the incidence of human suffering. But it would, at the same time, take away man's free will and make the world not better, but worse, for in such a recreated world there could be no hope of man's moral and spiritual progress. It is no good thinking that there could.

In face of the suffering that plagues human existence we may not avoid feeling at times that God the omnipotent could surely have contrived matters a little better.

Surely it was not impossible for Him to obtain the same end (of man's moral and spiritual progress) without employing the same means (of a world in which the risk of suffering occupies so prominent a place). But it *was* impossible. On any other basis man would not have been man. Human freedom involves the risk of error and of suffering, but it is essential to humanity. Without it we would be different creatures.

God could indeed have made the world one in which there could be no pain and no sin. But that would not have been an improved version of the world we know. It would have been a totally different world.

Football is reckoned by many to be a very good game. Millions find in it recreation and exercise, thrill and enjoyment. To the vast numbers of people participating, football is a beneficial thing which they would be very sorry to be without. Now, football is a manmade game with laws that have been devised to make it as good a game as possible. But accidents happen in this game. Often men sustain bruises. Sometimes men get broken limbs. Occasionally men have died. Despite this, men reckon it a good game and a desirable game and despite it, men still play it, not reluctantly but eagerly.

The possibility of hurt belongs to the very nature of the game as it is and the fact is that we cannot have the game without the risk. To eliminate the risk would mean making it a different game, and one which, few would doubt, would be much inferior.

Somewhat similarly, the world which God has created contains the ever-present risk of suffering and pain. But if that risk were removed the world would be a different world. Would it be a better world?

The Christian believes it would not. He believes that the world as it is, is the best world possible for the fulfillment of God's purposes of love.

Our stubborn minds may persist, "Surely this is a denial of God's omnipotence. Surely if God is an omnipotent Being, He could create a universe free from suffering in which it would still be possible for His purposes to be fulfilled."

This, however, is to misunderstand the omnipotence of God. Omnipotence does not mean the ability to do the impossible or to perform mutually contradictory actions at the same time.

A story—apocryphal, no doubt, but apposite here—is told of a Scottish Sunday School teacher who was speaking to her class of boys on the subject of God's omnipotence. In the course of her talk she was moved to say, "God can do anything at all. There is nothing that He can't do." And then she added, in an attempt to drive home her point with perhaps more zeal than wisdom, "Can you think of anything that God could not do?"

At once one of her scholars replied, "Please, Miss, God coudna' mak' oor Jock's mooth ony bigger withoot shiftin' his lugs." (God could not make our Jock's mouth any bigger without moving his ears.)

"Omnipotence does not mean the capacity to accomplish contradictions or absurdities; God's 'omnipotence' means power to do all that is intrinsically possible, not to do the intrinsically impossible. You may attribute miracles to Him but not nonsense."[3] God could not make square circles or hairless beards. And He cannot make free human personalities without allowing them free will.

More than that. The operation of God's omnipotence is conditioned by His nature. In one sense it is true that He is powerful enough to do anything at all. But in the most real sense He is able to do only what is good and wise and loving. For love's sake God must bestow on mankind the gift of free will, for only so can He create the possibility of souls fit for Heaven and eternal fellowship with Himself. That possibility cannot exist apart from mankind's possession of free will with its attendant hazards of sin and suffering.

In the best world possible there must be the risk of suffering. But this is a testimony to God's love, not a denial of it. It is not because He does not love us but because He does, that God has made the world one in which suffering may occur.

Let us suppose that I have a child just coming to the toddling stage and that I love him. When he comes to the point of taking his first steps on his own, what do I do? I have the power to prevent his walking on his own, and since I love him, I do not want him to fall and be hurt. But, since I love him, I also want him to learn to walk. I know that he must, or else he will not, cannot, grow into the complete man I want him to be. I therefore permit him to walk on his own with all the attendant risk of sustaining hurt. I permit that risk, not because I do not love my child, but because I do.

It is in a way not altogether dissimilar to this that, for love of us, God must restrain himself and allow the possibility of suffering in this world which the Christian believes to be the best of all possible worlds for His loving purposes.

NOTES

1. D'Arcy, *The Pain of This World and The Providence of God,* pp. 5, 6.
2. J. S. Whale, *The Problem of Evil,* p. 41.
3. C. S. Lewis, *The Problem of Pain,* p. 16.

· 3 ·

"Sent" by God?

I WENT one day to a hospital ward to see a young man, devoutly Christian, who had been involved in a road accident. His foot had been amputated and I was full of sympathy for a lad, full of life and keen on games, who had become so sadly handicapped.

When I reached his bedside and murmured some words to indicate my sympathy, he replied with a smile, "Well, this is God's will for me and that's all there is to it."

I was deeply moved by the depth and sincerity of his faith. But I could not help thinking—as I still do—that his theology was shocking. I find it impossible to equate the picture of the God revealed in Jesus Christ with the picture of a Being who could say, "This healthy and active boy must lose his foot."

But that young man's remark and outlook are not uncommon. On the contrary, I can recall a whole catalogue of occasions of a parallel nature in my own experience.

I think, for instance, of a family of mother, father, and daughter. No more faithful Christian family could be imagined. In her mid-teens the daughter took ill and died. A few years later the mother also died and shortly afterwards the father, too—and so, faithful Christians all, the whole family was wiped out without even one of them approaching old age.

Someone said to me on the occasion of the third death, "It's terribly sad. But it is God's will and we must bear it." Was it God's will? When we think of Jesus and His revelation of the loving Heavenly Father, can we accept such a tragedy as the will of God, at least in the sense of His deliberate decree?

I think of a lad, healthy, active, and with a keen zest for living, who fell ill with leukemia and in a few short weeks was dead. He was seventeen.

I think of a young mother whose baby was born so badly deformed that in the week or two he survived she was not permitted to see him.

I think of another young mother whose baby was born severely mentally retarded but lived for years, needing constant strength-sapping, heartrending attention for all those many functions which normal people perform as a matter of course.

I think of a bright-faced young man, recently standing before me as a bridegroom, who was killed in an air crash. I think of a young handicapped woman whose clothes were set alight to make her a human torch and who died some little time and some great suffering later. I think of many other tragic things in my own experience, but the examples cited are already enough to make my point.

The point is this. In every one of these instances someone said, "It is the will of God." And in every single instance I refuse to accept that verdict. As God is made known to me in Jesus Christ, I am forced to the conclusion that the very nature of the case denies every time that this could have been God's will, at least in the sense of his choice or preference. To say that God would deliberately rob a young wife of her husband or rob a small boy of his sight or a little girl of her health represents God as a monster, rather than the loving Father Jesus has shown Him to be. Yet this is just what we are saying when we ascribe the calamities of life to the will of God in the sense of his deliberate decree.

We attribute to God things which, if they were the doing of a human father, would shock us and disgust us. It is surely much more shocking to suggest that they are the doing of a Heavenly Father whose nature is love. Many of us need to have our thinking straightened out and our theology put to rights on this matter.

Look at it this way. We say, "God's will. God's will. God's will," in face of suffering. But when a loved one falls sick or has an accident, what do we do? Most likely, we send posthaste for the doctor. And why do we send for the doctor? So that he might make our loved one well again. But if his illness or injury are decreed by God, why send for the doctor at all? Why not just leave it with God?

Doctors' lives are a constant warfare against illness, disease, and accident. Would anyone suggest that they are fighting against God? Of course not. Everyone would agree that doctors in their work are on the side of God.

Think of Jesus for a moment. When He was on earth He did not look on suffering and its various manifestations as the will of God in the sense that they were God's desire. He clearly regarded these things as the enemies of life at its best and spent a lot of His time combating them in individual experience.

It is wrong to think that our troubles are wished on us by God. When tragedy befalls us, all that we are entitled to say is, not, "God has decreed this" but "God has permitted this." God does not send these things but has put us in a world where such things may happen and often do.

God would wish for us only what is good. But two factors frequently get in the way of that wish. The first of these is that this world is one in which natural law operates and its processes may lead to things like earthquake, flood, and fire. Some of the catastrophes that overtake human life find their origin here.

Many more find their origin in the second factor, man's possession of free will and the consequent possibility of his making wrong choices. Much of human suffering is traceable directly or remotely to human ignorance or human folly or human sin. (I do not mean that suffering is always the sufferer's own fault. Very often the innocent suffers for another's guilt, as, for instance, when a child is born maimed or sickly because of a parent's venereal disease. But this is a matter to which we will return.)

These two factors mean that frequently suffering breaks in upon human experience—upon the lives of the good and the kind just as much as upon the bad and the cruel. And when it does, although He has not decreed the particular occurrences and does not desire them, God permits it.

If such things are not the wish of God and yet, as is demonstrable, happen with heartrending frequency, does this mean that God is powerless to prevent them? Here the classical antithesis between God's love and God's omnipotence threatens to reappear.

It is not, however, a true antithesis. The situation is that God's omnipotence is restricted, *voluntarily* restricted, by the demands of His love.

Some undesirable things, or at least their possibility, must be allowed in order that the purposes of love may have scope to work themselves out. That is to say, God does not "send" suffering in the sense with which we began this chapter. He allows its possibility and it is in this sense only that suffering is the will of God.

Let me try to illustrate.

When we look at Jesus Christ in the belief that in Him God is perfectly revealed, it is plain that God's wish for the nations of the world must be that they should live at peace together and in a condition of amity and concord. But when, by virtue of human sin and folly, nations go to war against each other, God *permits* this and permits the consequences of war, permits bullets to plow through human flesh and bombs to destroy places and people. God allows this, but neither decrees it nor desires it.

If a man sits at the wheel of his motor car with the sharpness of his reflexes blunted by alcohol and a child darts across his path, too near him for his slowed-down faculties to avoid collision, God permits that child to be struck, perhaps to be seriously hurt or even killed. God does not decree that this should happen. But when man's folly combines with natural law to produce a certain result, no matter how appalling, normally God permits it to come about.

Does, then, God "permit" in the sense that He creates the world and makes its rules and then is relegated to the role of mere, though undoubtedly interested, spectator? Not at all. God retains His sovereignty and could intervene at any time if He wished. But to make a practice of so doing would produce chaos instead of order and would deprive man of that freedom of will which is essential to the development of his soul. (Or, at least, it would destroy the reality of his freedom in as much as he would be miraculously safeguarded from the consequences of any and every wrong action.)

The situation is this. Supposing a man steps abruptly off the sidewalk into the path of an oncoming bus. God has the power to intervene and arrest the onward progress of the bus and so preserve the man from injury, but He is extremely unlikely to do any such thing. To do so would be to break his own established laws and to make a habit of acting in this way would be for God to have made a world of order and then to have replaced the order with anarchy.

So usually things are allowed to take their course, their orderly, law-abiding course. And it could not be other than this without the world becoming a different place, and an inferior one at that, in which it would no longer be possible for God's loving purposes for men to be accomplished.

Supplementary questions no doubt spring to mind. For instance, it may be asked, "If you deny the belief that God 'sends' suffering, do you not at the same time deny, to some at least, a source of comfort when suffering comes?"

There is point in this. It is true that many have been comforted in time of suffering by their belief that this was what their loving Father had decreed for them. It might be agonizing, it might be difficult to understand, but it was visited upon them by God and, therefore, for some good, if inscrutable, purpose—and this belief went some way toward helping them to bear it.

If I were to come to these people and say to them in the context of their suffering, "Your belief is erroneous. God does not *send* your suffering—not at least in the fashion that you have been imagining. Suffering is simply one of the hazards of this world and for you the hazard has become an actuality," would I not be in danger of knocking away a prop that is helping to support them against total collapse?

Of course I would. But, then, I never would come to such a person in his actual time of suffering and dispute his theological understanding of it. When, for instance, I sat beside the hospital bed where this chapter began and heard my friend say of his smashed and amputated foot, "It was the will of God," I was careful to offer no criticism of the theology of his statement, deeply though I deplored it. Undoubtedly it would be wrong to dispute this belief with any man while he was actually suffering. Although you know a man's house to be ill-founded and vulnerable to tempest, there is little wisdom in trying to rebuild it for him in the midst of a storm. Once the storm has struck, you must just wait in the hope and the prayer that the house will survive, and then get ahead with the job of rebuilding once the sun breaks through again, lest the next storm prove too much.

At the same time, two other comments must be made. It is true that many people have found comfort in the belief that their suffering is "sent" by God. But this is only a partial statement of the case, for a man cannot possibly find the deepest or the most enduring kind of comfort in what is at best only a half truth. Comfort of a sort comes to many men and women through their belief that God has willed their suffering. But they would have even greater comfort if they realized that God does not send their suffering but merely allows it and that He is both sharing it with them and offering help to face it.

The second comment is this. Many have found comfort in holding to the belief that suffering is due to God's specific decree. But in at least as many cases that same belief has caused distress and sometimes even loss of faith. It is the cause of as much harm as good, and probably more.

I know a girl who was brought up to say her prayers every night, and every night she used to say, among other things, "Lord, look after my mummy and daddy and keep them safe." One night their house caught on fire, suddenly, swiftly, and dreadfully—and in the blaze her father was killed and her mother badly injured. That young girl was left not only with the agonizing heartache of the tragic misfortune that had come upon her parents. She was left also with great bewilderment of mind and great distress of spirit because of her belief that God had decreed this tragedy in spite of her nightly prayer. Her faith, indeed, was shattered.

Many similar instances could be quoted where such a view of suffering has led to a straining or actual breaking of faith.

While the "will of God" view of suffering is a source of some comfort to many, there is much more to be said on the other side. The truth in this instance is not only more desirable for its own sake, but is, in fact, more helpful than the partial truth which is its substitute in so many minds.

Let me sum up what this chapter has tried to say.

Suffering is not the will of God in the sense that God decrees that a particular tragedy shall happen at a particular time. God has made a world in which the possibility of suffering exists and when that possibility becomes a reality, He normally allows it, not because He wills it so but because the constitution of the world demands it.

Far from being the deliberate wish of God, the bulk of human suffering is traceable to man's own sin or folly. C. S. Lewis says:

> The possibility of pain is inherent in the very existence of a world where souls can meet. When souls become wicked they will certainly use this possibility to hurt one another; and this, perhaps, accounts for four-fifths of the sufferings of men. It is men, not God, who have produced racks, whips, prisons, slavery, guns, bayonets and bombs; it is by human avarice or human stupidity,

not by the churlishness of nature, that we have poverty and overwork.[1]

Not all of human suffering, of course, can be traced to man's misuse of his free will in this way. Some belongs entirely to the realm of the world as it is and the laws that govern it.

The world as it is, with its law and order and man's possession of free will—carrying with them, as they do, the risk of suffering—is, we believe, the best possible world for God's loving purpose, the salvation of men. This, however, is a far cry from the belief that our suffering is sent by God. "If I give my boy a pair of roller skates, I immediately make it possible for him to get a bad bump. That is a very different thing from taking him by the neck and banging his head upon the ground."[2]

NOTES

1. C. S. Lewis, *The Problem of Pain,* p. 77.
2. L. Weatherhead, *Why Do Men Suffer?* p. 126.

· 4 ·

Punishment for Sin?

A CONSIDERABLE number of people believe that all suffering is punishment for wrongdoing. That is, life metes out to us what we deserve.

This was a very early and persistent Old Testament idea. The people of Israel believed firmly that God punished iniquity and rewarded righteousness. Look, for example, at Deuteronomy 11:26–28: "Behold, I set before you this day a blessing and a curse: the blessing, if you obey the commandments of the Lord your God, which I command you this day. And the curse, if you do not obey the commandments of the Lord your God." Or at Jeremiah 17:5–8, 10:

> Thus says the Lord: "Cursed is the man who trusts in man and makes flesh his arm, whose heart turns away from the Lord. He is like a shrub in the desert, and shall not see any good come. He shall dwell in the parched places of the wilderness, in an uninhabited salt land. Blessed is the man who trusts in the Lord, whose trust is the Lord. He is like a tree planted by water, that sends out its roots by the stream, and does not fear when heat comes, for its leaves remain green, and is not anxious in the year of drought, for it does not cease to bear fruit ... I the Lord search the mind and try the heart, to give to every man according to his ways, according to the fruit of his doings."

The view illustrated in these passages is that God would inevitably punish evil and reward good and that He would do so in this world. This, of course, was how it had to be. If He were to punish and reward, the present was the only sphere in which He could do so. For there was none beyond it. In the main, the Jews of Old Testament times had no real conception of life beyond this world. It was not until very late in the Old Testament period that there was any vision of life hereafter and even then it was confined to fragmentary glimpses.

So then, the characteristic and predominant view of the people of the Old Testament was that God assigned weal or woe to men according to their merits and that He did so in this life. The literature of the Old Testament reflects this again and again.

Nowhere, perhaps, do we find it better illustrated than in the Psalms. The Psalms are the distillation of the deepest devotion and the most profoundly held beliefs of the Hebrews, and over and over again they give expression to the conviction that the good will prosper and the wicked suffer.

Psalm 112:1–3 is typical of many others: "Blessed is the man who fears the Lord, who greatly delights in his commandments! His descendants will be mighty in the land; the generation of the upright will be blessed. Wealth and riches are in his house; and his righteousness endures for ever."

Another is Psalm 128:

Blessed is every one who fears the Lord, who walks in his ways! You shall eat the fruit of the labor of your hands; you shall be happy, and it shall be well with you. Your wife will be like a fruitful vine within your house; your children will be like olive shoots around your table.

Lo, thus shall the man be blessed who fears the Lord.
The Lord bless you from Zion! May you see the prosperity of Jerusalem all the days of your life! May you
see your children's children! Peace be upon Israel!

The assertion that God would protect and prosper the
good man carried with it the implication that God would
punish the evildoer. This implication is not quite so frequently given explicit expression, but, when it is, it is just
as emphatically expressed as, for example, in Psalm 32:10:
"Many are the pangs of the wicked" and in Psalm 91:8:
"You will only look with your eyes and see the recompense
of the wicked."

At the same time many Psalms take cognizance of the
fact that often the wicked do prosper—or apparently so—
and the good suffer. These Psalms assert that, even
though the evildoer may seem to be having success and
prosperity, this happy state will be his only for a time. In
the end—it may be sooner, it may be later—punishment
will overtake him, his prosperity will vanish, and suffering
befall him. So we have Psalm 37:1, 2, for instance, saying:
"Fret not yourself because of the wicked, be not envious of
wrongdoers! For they will soon fade like the grass, and
wither like the green herb."

The good man may suffer for a time and the evil man
may prosper for a time. But these injustices are temporary
things. In the end God puts them to rights and both good
and bad receive their just desserts.

Although the Psalms are, in the main, not unrealistic
in their doctrine of divine retribution—namely, that it
may be ultimate rather than immediate—nevertheless the
dominant idea among the Hebrews was that a man always
"got what he deserved." Everything that befell a man was
meted out to him by God according to the kind of man he

had shown himself to be. Which meant, in particular, that all suffering was God's punishment for sin.

Even in the great biblical drama of Job we find this conception reflected. It was not the view of the writer nor the teaching of his book. But it clearly emerges that this was the commonly held opinion.

Job is a man of God, as is demonstrated by his great prosperity. But suddenly the sky darkens for him. He is stricken with a series of calamities that affect his possessions, his family, and his person, and everyone assumes that this must be the consequence of sin.

His friends say to him: "You must have done something very bad to deserve this. What was it?" Job denies their accusation and insists that he is as much a man of God still as ever he was in the days of his prosperity. His friends will not listen to his protestations. His suffering makes the matter self-evident. He must have sinned and sinned badly—how otherwise can his calamities be explained?

In the end, of course, the book repudiates the assumption that Job's suffering must be the consequence of sin and assigns to it a disciplinary character. We will return to this later, but our point meantime is that the book of Job illustrates how prevalent was the idea that suffering was the penalty for sin and usually for a man's own sin at that.

This conception carried over into New Testament times. We find evidence of it, for example, in the incident recorded in the ninth chapter of the fourth Gospel: "As Jesus passed by, he saw a man blind from his birth. And his disciples asked him, 'Rabbi, who sinned, this man or his parents, that he was born blind?' " (John 9:1, 2).

Leaving aside the difficulty of conceiving how the man, if blind *from birth,* could be personally responsible for his blindness, the fact remains that the disciples' question makes plain how generally it was assumed that there was a close causal connection between suffering and sin.

Jesus, of course, firmly rebutted the assumption on that occasion as on others. Despite this, the idea has persisted into the Christian Church and is not uncommon even today. Not infrequently, for instance, a parent may be heard to counsel a child: "If you do not behave yourself, God will punish you," or, when some misdemeanor results in a minor accident, "That is what you get for being naughty. God has punished you."

What is even more frequent is to hear someone say in circumstances of suffering, "What have I done to deserve this?" No one, perhaps, hears this kind of utterance more often than the Christian minister. Disaster comes in some form or another and when the minister calls to try and give comfort, the sufferer says to him, "I must have done something really wicked to be suffering like this." Or someone to whom the sufferer is very near and dear says, with more than a trace of bitterness, "I am sure X has done nothing to deserve this. I cannot understand why he is having to suffer so."

Still today in the minds of many people the underlying idea is that suffering and freedom from suffering are matters of strict merit, dispensed by God according to a rigid standard of punishment for the evildoer and blessing for the well-behaved. And still the attempt is made to argue this point of view. Stanley Jones tells, for instance, how, "In Burma a severe earthquake shook down everything but left a Christian's house standing in the midst of it, and this was considered an act of Providence."[1]

Even today one will often hear this kind of thing quoted in support of the theory that people get what they deserve. But this is to adopt a totally unrealistic attitude to the facts. For, as Stanley Jones says in the same paragraph, "It is simply not true that earthquakes hit the bad and spare the good. An earthquake in India shook down a mission building and left a brothel standing nearby."[2] The fact is that the godly man is just as liable to suffer as the ungodly.

In Matthew Arnold's words:

> Earthquakes do not scorn
> The just man to entomb,
> Nor lightning stand aside
> To find his virtues room:
> Nor is that wind less rough that
> blows a good man's barge.

It must be recognized, however, that there *is* a retributive quality about much of the suffering in the world. Sin does carry inevitable consequences with it and bring relentless suffering in its train. This is a demonstrable fact (although the unpleasant consequences are not always for the perpetrator of the sin only and sometimes, it may seem, not for him at all).

Here, for instance, is a man who has contracted venereal disease and this is directly traceable to his sexual promiscuity. Here is another man who has become ill with cirrhosis of the liver and this is directly caused by his excessive drinking over a period of years. Here is yet another whose prosperous business begins to totter and finally collapses in ruins and the reason is to be found in an increasing indulgence of selfish pleasures accompanied by an increasing neglect of business affairs.

Such instances could be multiplied. Often suffering is quite obviously the penalty incurred by a man's sin or folly.

This statement, however, must be speedily qualified. It is true that much suffering may be reckoned as the consequence of sin. But it is by no means an inflexible rule that the guilty suffer in this life—or that the innocent do not.

Here, for instance, is a man who has all his days lived a clean and wholesome life and now he is struck down by cancer which takes him off, after prolonged pain, to an early grave. Here is another man who is as conscientiously attentive to his business as could be imagined and yet his business fails. Here is another who is of the sweetest temper and most placid disposition and yet is struck down suddenly and severely with coronary thrombosis.

Nor is suffering, even when it is the consequence of sin, punishment in the sense of something meted out by God in direct response to the sin committed. If we were to try to construe suffering in this way we would soon find ourselves involved in the impossible task of offering a satisfactory explanation of what would appear to be its frequent unjust apportioning.

What do we really mean, then, when we say that much suffering is of a retributive character? We mean that a great deal of human suffering comes about because of the principle of cause and effect that underlies the constitution of the world. For this is a world of natural and moral law; and built into its structure is the rule that if someone breaks the law, then someone—not necessarily the same someone—is liable to be hurt.

This principle lies at the very heart of the Old Testament law books and many of their regulations. It is this principle that leads these books, for instance, to assert that God will visit "the iniquity of the fathers upon the children to the third and fourth generation of those who hate me"

(Exodus 20:5). This statement displays a clear grasp of the truth that sin brings inevitable suffering in its wake, even in this present world—and, if it is not as the direct decree of God which the quotation would suggest but rather as a consequence of God's world being as it is, it is no less inevitable because of that. The suffering may not be immediate and it may not befall the one who committed the sin. But it will follow and, when it comes, it may endure for a long time.

And it is in this way that much of human suffering finds its origin. Retribution, it is true, but a far cry from the idea of a half-pound of suffering being weighed out in return for a half-pound of evildoing.

NOTES

1. S. Jones, *Christ and Human Suffering*, p. 27.
2. *Ibid.*, pp. 26–27.

· 5 ·

Some Further Questions

Is Suffering Disciplinary?

OUR CONSIDERATION of suffering as punishment leads us naturally to a consideration of suffering as discipline.

The view of suffering finally presented by the book of Job was that Job's suffering was a test of faith. When his disasters began to come upon him, his friends said, "This is punishment for sin. You must have sinned badly." Their verdict was in line with the current conception of suffering as being completely and directly retributive. But Job vehemently denied this reading of the events and insisted that he had committed no sin worthy of such punishment. In this situation—suffering grievously, although convinced that his suffering was quite undeserved, and all this against the background of a theology which linked suffering and merit very closely—Job was very much open to the temptation to abandon faith on the score that God was being grossly unfair to him. In the event, however, he resisted the temptation.

The happenings in which Job found himself so painfully embroiled were, we discover, part of a conflict between God and Satan. Satan had asserted that Job continued faithful only because he was prosperous and that adversity would lead to an abandonment of his faith. God, on the other hand, was sure that Job's faith was more securely based than that. In this confidence, He gave Satan authority to test Job with misfortune and calamity. In the end, Job emerged from the trial with his faith not only intact but all the stronger for his experience.

Like the conception of suffering as a punishment, this idea of suffering as a divinely sponsored test of faith also persists into our own day. (How often, for example, does someone say, "These things are sent to try us."?) And, indeed, there is no doubt that frequently the experience of suffering does act as a test and does produce a strengthening of faith. But it could never seriously be suggested that this was the purpose, the *raison d'être*, of suffering. How, for example, could the suffering of a little child be made to fit this pattern?

It is a variant form of this view and a more persistent one that sees in suffering something that God intends as a means of *discipline*. Many times in the Old Testament we meet the idea of God sending suffering to a man for the specific purpose of teaching him some particular truth or of developing in him some particular virtue. Here are two examples: "I shall not die, but I shall live, and recount the deeds of the Lord. The Lord has chastened me sorely, but he has not given me over to death" (Psalm 118:17–18). And "My son, do not despise the Lord's discipline or be weary of his reproof, for the Lord reproves him whom he loves, as a father the son in whom he delights" (Proverbs 3:11–12). It is a not unfamiliar idea in the New Testament, too, as, for example, in Hebrews 12:5–7:

> Have you forgotten the exhortation which addresses you as sons?—"My son, do not regard lightly the discipline of the Lord, nor lose courage when you are punished by him. For the Lord disciplines him whom he loves, and chastises every son whom he receives." It is for discipline that you have to endure. God is treating you as sons; for what son is there whom his father does not discipline?

Nor is the notion at all uncommon in the present day.

It is beyond doubt that good effects may issue from the experience of suffering. Many times a man has been forced back through suffering upon the things that really count and brought face to face with reality; and it has often happened that through undergoing an experience of suffering a man's qualities of character have been refined and improved. But this is a different thing from saying that God apportions a quota of suffering in order to produce a good result; and again we may ask how such a theory is to explain the suffering of a little child.

In any case, while the experience of suffering may produce a good result, this by no means always happens. Just as often suffering produces a bad result. Many a man is driven by suffering to a bitter disavowal of God. Many a man emerges from suffering with his character much the poorer.

What do we mean, then, if we say that there is a disciplinary aspect to suffering? We mean this. There is a way of meeting suffering which can lead to its being overruled to a worthwhile end.

That is to say, suffering is not of itself the producer of good. Suffering in itself is evil and contrary to God's real desire for men. But out of the evil of suffering, when met in the right way, good may come.

What this amounts to is that suffering has a possible disciplinary effect, not a necessary one. A man *may* emerge from the experience of suffering the better for his experience. But there is no guarantee that he *will*. So far as the discipline of a man's character and soul is concerned, suffering is neutral, of itself on the side neither of God nor of the Devil. It is the attitude a man adopts to his suffering that is the determinative factor.

Is Suffering Necessary for Man's Development?

We noted earlier that suffering is never directly decreed by God. It is God's will only in the sense that He permits it to happen, and this because the risk of suffering is an integral part of what is the best world possible for God's loving purposes.

This raises a question supplementary to the one we have just been considering. Is suffering necessary to a man's full development? Does God require suffering in order to fulfill His loving purposes?

The answer is "No." The experience of suffering is not needed before a man can become what God means and desires him to be. Otherwise it would mean that God needed the help of evil in order to produce good. This would do little credit to God and is manifestly absurd.

It is the *possibility* of suffering, not its *actuality*, that is necessary. It is not that suffering *must* happen but that suffering *may* happen. Let me try to illustrate by renewing the comparison with the game of football.

This is a very popular game. Many thousands derive a great deal of pleasure from playing it. Now people sometimes are injured playing football and, on occasion, the injury may be very painful or even extremely serious. That this should happen is not the purpose of the game, but the risk of it could not be eliminated without radically altering the nature of the game. The *fact* of hurt is not necessary to make the game what it is meant to be; but the *risk* is.

So, too, the possibility of suffering, rather than its actuality, is necessary for the development of man's personality and the fulfillment of his destiny.

Do Sin and Folly Matter?

We saw that, given the proper response on the part of the sufferer, God could turn any suffering to good account. It might appear from this that it does not really matter whether a man is sinful or foolish. If God is going to over-rule everything to a good end anyway, what is the difference?

This attitude is neither new nor uncommon. It was well known to the apostle Paul, who decisively dealt with it. For example: "What shall we say then? Are we to continue in sin that grace may abound? By no means! How can we who died to sin still live in it?" (Romans 6: 1–2).

There is no need to try to restate Paul's case. I merely make one or two observations.

For one thing, we must not ignore the fact that, even though God should overrule an evil thing to a good end, this does not change its character. It remains just as evil as it was.

Moreover, we have not said that God will always bring good out of evil but that He can and will, when given the proper response—which is much different from saying that out of every bad situation good will come.

This adds up to a reaffirmation of the Pauline emphasis that sin is sin whatever the grace of God may do with it. It is not something to be regarded as trivial or inconsequential. It is something whose enormity is revealed by the Cross of Christ, which is what it cost God to deal with it.

So far I have been speaking in this section about sin and evil generally, although our primary concern in this book is with suffering, but no doubt the implications with regard to suffering will be clear.

While the grace of God may often—given the right response—bring blessing out of suffering, this does not make suffering a good thing in itself or something to be desired. It does not even make it something to be complacently tolerated, least of all in other people.

The fact that suffering may be overruled to a good end provides us with neither the slightest reason nor the flimsiest excuse for doing nothing either to alleviate it or to remove it. Later in this book I am going to suggest that the real answer to the problem of suffering is to be found in the victory offered by the Christian Gospel. But this does not mean that our sole responsibility with regard to suffering is to proclaim this message. This may be the most important single thing to do. But we are not to think that having done this, we have done all we might or ought.

Stanley Jones tells this story: "A wealthy farmer prayed in his family circle that his unfortunate neighbors might not starve. When they arose from their knees, his little girl said to him, 'Daddy, you needn't have bothered God with that, for *you* can quite easily keep them from starving.'"

That story makes the point very clearly. Everyone may make a contribution, individual and corporate, toward the reduction of suffering, and the correction or elimination of the circumstances that cause it. Our particular contribution may be calling in the doctor without delay or enlisting hospital care; it may be teaching our children personal hygiene or crusading for better housing. It may be one or more of a hundred things. But it will be a refusal to regard suffering as either necessary or desirable. Because in God's sight it is neither.

Is God Sympathetic?

Does God feel with us or for us in our suffering?

The "Preacher" of the Book of Ecclesiastes would have been in no two minds about the answer.

To him, suffering was the capricious visitation of a God who had no standards, far less sympathy. The Preacher took it for granted that all suffering was sent by God and he could discover neither rhyme nor reason in the sending of it. He gives forcible expression to his disgust more than once. In Ecclesiastes 9:2–3, for example, he says: "And for all men alike there is one fate, for just and unjust, good and bad, pure and impure, for him who sacrifices and for him who never sacrifices; as with the good man so with the sinner; the profane man fares like the man whose oath is sacred. There is no evil like this in the world, that all men have one fate." (Moffatt)

So far as the Preacher is concerned, suffering is something dispensed by God in completely arbitrary fashion. Ecclesiastes has a most cynical and pessimistic view of life. It does not doubt the existence of God and it believes that He exercises detailed control of men's lives. But God is quite haphazard and unpredictable in His treatment of individual men.

This view of God's dealings with men is similar to that expressed in Robert Browning's *Caliban upon Setebos:*

> Am strong myself compared to yonder crabs
> That march now from the mountain to the sea;
> Let twenty pass, and stone the twenty-first,
> Loving not, hating not, just choosing so.
> Say, the first straggler that boasts purple spots
> Shall join the file, one pincer twisted off;
> Say this bruised fellow shall receive a worm,
> And two worms he whose nippers end in red;
> As it likes me each time, I do; So He. . . .

The Ecclesiastes view of God as the direct and arbitrary dispenser of a man's suffering, carrying with it the inevitable corollary that He must be totally without sympathy toward suffering men, could well be discounted merely on the score of its naïveté. But in any case the New Testament quite precludes such a notion, for it clearly pictures God as One who suffers with His suffering people.

The assertion of the Epistle to the Hebrews that we have in Jesus a high priest who is "able to sympathize with our weaknesses" may, it is true, refer to His sympathy with our frailties rather than with our sufferings. Nevertheless, the sense of compassion toward our griefs and pains in which it is popularly accepted is the sense of many another sentence and paragraph in the New Testament. We are given to see there, through Jesus Christ, a God who, far from being a cruel, capricious distributor of woes or even an unfeeling witness of them, enters with real concern into our every experience of suffering.

One of the most deeply moving (as well as most sternly challenging) sayings of Jesus is that in Matthew 25:40:"Truly, I say to you, as you did it to one of the least of these my brethren, you did it to me." Here we find Jesus declaring that He is in some very real fashion involved with every one of life's sufferers. When suffering overtakes us, whatever it be and however much it may or may not be our own fault, God in Christ is close beside us, sharing the pain.

This is the answer of Christian belief to the question with which we began—"Is God sympathetic?—and it is summed up in this English translation of a medieval Latin verse:

> Think not thou canst sigh a sigh,
> And thy Maker is not nigh.
> Think not thou canst weep a tear,
> And thy Maker is not near.
> Oh! He gives to us His joy

That our grief He may destroy,
Till our grief is past and gone
He doth sit by us and moan.

How About Natural Catastrophe?

This chapter is an attempt to tidy up some of the loose ends rather obviously left by our consideration so far of the "Why?" side of the problem of suffering. One of these is the question of natural catastrophe. How do things like earthquake, fire, and flood fit in to the pattern we have been trying to weave concerning the occurrence of human suffering—if, indeed, they fit in at all?

What we have said so far is that the risk of suffering is a constituent part of the world as it is, a world which we believe to be the best world possible for God's loving purposes. God does not decree an individual's suffering. He would, indeed, wish it not to happen and enters into the situation with real compassion when it does. However, the possibility—although not the actuality—of suffering is necessary to make this a world in which a man may fulfill his intended destiny; and often that possibility becomes actual fact. When it does, it is often because of man's misuse of his free will and, in fact, a great deal of human suffering is to be accounted for in this way.

But it is just here that the problem of natural catastrophe is most acutely focused. There are calamities of nature which cannot be laid at the door of human responsibility. What are we to say of them? Might not a loving, omnipotent God have so constructed His universe that they at least were eliminated?

The fact seems to be that such things, too, belong, and unavoidably belong, to this "best world possible." They come about because this is a world of law and, as we saw already, a world which was lawless would not be a world fit to live in. Wheeler Robinson affirms that natural calamities such as earthquake, volcano, storm, flood, frost, avalanche, epidemic, and endemic diseases

> belong to Nature's regularity. Their appearance is often sudden and catastrophic, but they are the result of long preparation. The storm that destroys a harvest and brings famine is as much the regular product of meteorological law as the harvest it destroys is the product of agricultural law. It would be an enormous boon to mankind if the malaria mosquito could be exterminated and civilization wage successful warfare against the microorganism that causes malignant cholera. Yet these enemies of man are exceptional products of a biological order which is the condition of our life.[1]

This answer may seem too glib for some and yet I believe it true. It does not make the reality and the terror of these things any less harsh. But it saves us from the heartrending folly of blaming them upon God's lack of love.

Does the Bible Give a Ready-made Answer?

The teaching of Scripture has underlain all our attempts in this book to grapple with the problem of suffering, and on more than one occasion we have taken a look at a particular passage. Nevertheless, even though it must involve a measure of repetition, it may be worth while to make a brief summary now of some of the Bible's specific comments on suffering.

We must not, however, expect the Bible to provide us with a quick, simple, and easy-to-digest solution. We make a very disappointing mistake if we imagine that this, or any major problem for that matter, is likely to find a facile answer in the application of a Scripture text.

After a series of broadcast talks on our present problem, J. S. Whale received a number of letters telling him that he would have found a quicker and more satisfactory answer simply by looking up this text or that. But we cannot really expect it to be so easy as that. For, as Whale points out, the Bible cannot properly be read "in the flat" like this and we find, for example, that the Old Testament offers "at least five distinct and different answers to the problem of suffering." Whale goes on to say that, "We use the Bible rightly only when, to quote Luther, we see that it is the cradle wherein Christ is laid; that is, when we worship the Holy Child and not His crib."[2]

Keeping this word of caution in mind, we look first at the chief Old Testament ideas on the subject of human suffering.

The dominant Old Testament understanding of suffering is that it was punishment. To begin with, this punishment was considered to be of a corporate kind. A family or group suffered, by way of retribution, for the sins of a member. When, for example, the widow of Sarephta's son died, she assumed that it must be because of some sin of hers. "After this the son of the woman, the mistress of the house, became ill; and his illness was so severe that there was no breath left in him. So she said to Elijah, 'What have you against me, O man of God? You have come to me to bring my sin to remembrance, and to cause the death of my son!'" (1 Kings 17:17–18).

Alongside the idea of corporate responsibility and retribution, although never so strong, we find also at times that of individual responsibility and retribution. We find it, for example, even in the Pentateuch—as, for instance, in Deuteronomy 24:16, "The fathers shall not be put to death for the children, nor shall the children be put to death for the fathers; every man shall be put to death for his own sin." This more advanced idea of individual punishment receives its most clear expression in Ezekiel. But even in Ezekiel the idea of corporate responsibility exists, too. And, despite Ezekiel, the idea long persisted among the Jews that people are punished for the sins of their parents.

Several Psalms give vigorous expression to the belief that God rewards the good and punishes the wicked. This is thought of as happening in this life, although not always immediately. Some Psalms, too, speak of suffering as having a disciplinary or remedial purpose.

As for the outlook of Job we simply quote these words from E. F. Sutcliffe: "The book of Job both transcends the older Old Testament conception of suffering and yet remains within it. It transcends it in that it definitely teaches that suffering may in God's providence fall on a good man to test the validity of his virtue. . . . The book yet remains within the purview of the Old Testament in that the story ends . . . in the renewed prosperity of the sufferer."[3]

Not a few traces of the Old Testament viewpoints are to be met in the pages of the New Testament.

We find, for instance, suffering regarded as punishment for sin. Zechariah is punished with temporary loss of speech because of his unwillingness to believe the promise of the angel (Luke 1:20). Herod's sudden death is attributed to his failure to give proper recognition to God's sovereignty (Acts 12:21–23). Elymas the sorcerer is struck blind for his machinations against the purposes of God (Acts 13:8–11).

The idea that suffering is a testing and a strengthening of faith is also encountered, most particularly in Hebrews 12:5–7, "My son, do not regard lightly the discipline of the Lord, nor lose courage when you are punished by him. For the Lord disciplines him whom he loves, and chastises every son whom he receives. It is for discipline that you have to endure."

The idea that all suffering was punishment for sin, either the sin of the sufferer or of someone else, confronted Jesus in the disciples' question of John 9:2, "Rabbi, who sinned, this man or his parents, that he was born blind?" Jesus immediately and categorically repudiated the idea by saying, "It was not that this man sinned, or his parents."

It was just as emphatically that He rejected the same notion when he spoke of Pilate's massacre of the Galileans and of the tragedy at Siloam:

> There were some present at that very time who told him of the Galileans whose blood Pilate had mingled with their sacrifices. And he answered them, "Do you think that these Galileans were worse sinners than all the other Galileans, because they suffered thus? I tell you, No. ... Or those eighteen upon whom the tower in Siloam fell and killed them, do you think that they were worse offenders than all the others who dwelt in Jerusalem? I tell you, No." (Luke 13:1–2, 4)

Of all the attitudes to suffering that the Bible reflects, that of Jesus must obviously be the most important; and it is plain that he did not regard it as punishment for sin nor as "sent" by God. He regarded it as something evil, the enemy of God and inimical to fullness of life, and so He sought to remove it wherever He could.

Nevertheless, the fact remains that Jesus does not give us much in the way of a theology or philosophy of suffering. Not even He offers us a ready-made answer to the problem of its existence. He offers, however, something much more important. He offers help in facing it.

NOTES

1. H. Wheeler Robinson, *Suffering, Human and Divine*, p. 112.
2. J. S. Whale, *The Problem of Evil*, pp. 78–79.
3. E. F. Sutcliffe, *Providence and Suffering in the Old and New Testaments*, p. 119.

· 6 ·

Some Alleviating
Considerations

OUR MAIN CONCERN so far has been with the "Why?" of
suffering and we have been endeavoring to find some explanation of its existence and of the perplexities that attend it. We must admit that we have been unable to
answer this question with anything like complete satisfaction. When we have said all that we have to say, much still
remains to puzzle and bewilder.

At the same time, this is neither less nor more than we
expected. We were careful to stress at the outset that we
did not hope to attain a fully adequate theory of suffering.
We hoped only to go some way toward answering its
"Why?" and perhaps in some measure ease the agony of
mind that accompanies the question. If we have done that,
we have justified the writing of this book so far.

We also stated at the beginning that we had another—
our chief—purpose in writing and that was to try to give
an answer to the even more important question of the
"How?" of suffering, how to face up to it without being
crushed. It is with this question we shall be concerned
from now on.

First of all, as a kind of bridge between the How and
the Why aspects of our study, we take account of some
considerations that may alleviate, for the Christian, the
distress of mind so often occasioned when he contem-

plates the fact of suffering side by side with the loving omnipotence of God.

Free Will

In this category stands, of course, the realization with which we have already dealt: that particular cases of suffering, so far from being sent by God, are often traceable to the agency of man. Much of human suffering is due, directly or indirectly, to man's misuse of his capacity for free choice.

Illustrations have been given and could be multiplied. But the point has already been sufficiently made. The first of our alleviating factors need not, therefore, detain us any longer.

The Hope of Heaven

The second alleviating factor is the Christian's assurance of "the life everlasting," his hope of Heaven. He believes that this world is not the whole story. It is no more than the opening chapter; further and greater chapters are to follow. The confident expectation of a better life beyond, where the shadows are dispelled and pain is no more, may go a long way toward enabling a man to endure with fortitude the most agonizing of suffering.

The New Testament strikes this note many times, as, for example, in Romans 8:18: "I consider that the sufferings of this present time are not worth comparing with the glory that is to be revealed to us." The joy in store for the Christian far outreaches any suffering that might befall in the meantime. Over and over again this consideration is brought forward in the New Testament books—books, let us remember, that were written often in face of a situation of suffering.

All down the Christian centuries since, the vision of Heaven has been one that has lightened the darkness of present sorrow and helped make the immediate burden more bearable.

An often told story of Robert Louis Stevenson relates how one day in Fife he came upon a man engaged on that messiest of jobs, "mucking a byre" (that is, cleaning the manure out of a cow barn). Stevenson, wondering how anyone could put up with such a task day after day, said to him, "Don't you get terribly sick of all this?" To which the man replied in words that have become immortal, "He that has aye something ayont need never weary."

The man who has always something in store need never be cast down. And the Christian hope of Heaven can sustain a man's heart in the worst of afflictions.

It must be admitted that, while this hope has been central to the Christian Gospel from the beginning, and, while from the New Testament onward it has occupied a prominent place in Christian thought and speech and writing, recently in some quarters there has been a tendency to look askance at any attempt to make much of it or to placard it so freely as used to be. "We are very shy nowadays of even mentioning heaven. We are afraid of the jeer about 'pie in the sky' and of being told that we are trying to 'escape' from the duty of making a happy world here and now into dreams of a happy world elsewhere."[1]

The fact, admittedly shameful, that Christians have at times neglected or ignored their responsibilities toward the improvement of this world and the fact that their opponents have made capital out of this with their jeers of "pie in the sky when you die" do not alter the truth of heaven, if indeed it is true. The Christian believes that it is and the confidence that heaven lies ahead may make a great difference to him in face of suffering.

The Limits of Human Understanding

Next is the fact of our limited human understanding. Many things concerning the world in general and the fact of human suffering in particular occasion much anguish of mind for no other reason than that our finite minds are just not capable of grasping the whole picture. Seeing only in part, we draw wrong conclusions.

Wheeler Robinson quotes the following story. A Christian missionary in China came into conflict with the evangelist of a native sect who was busily engaged in denouncing the Christian religion as cruel and inhuman. He challenged the native evangelist to substantiate the absurd charge he was making. Whereupon the other produced a medical missionary's book in which there were illustrations of surgical operations. Ignorant of the humane object of surgery, he regarded operations as proof of the cruelty of Christians.[2]

Many of our mental agonies over the question of suffering may be due to equally grotesque misjudgments of things we do not fully understand.

The traditional manner of making a Persian carpet may provide an apt illustration. It is erected vertically on a frame and on one side a number of boys are seated at different parts of the carpet and at different levels. On the other side is the master weaver. He calls out instructions to the boys and they each weave in their part of the pattern according to the guidance received from a man whose face they cannot see.

As the boys are able to see it, the design of the carpet is a complete mess, merely a collection of blotches and unsightly blobs. Looking at it from their viewpoint, it is hard to imagine that there is any sense about what each individual is having to do.

Theirs, however, is the wrong side from which to judge. When, at the end of the day's work, they get down from their stools and walk round to the master's side, they can see that there *is* a pattern being worked out, a thing of intelligence and beauty.

How different is their impression now. And how different it will be when we can view the pattern of this world and our involvement in God's purposes from "the other side." At the moment we are unable to comprehend the whole pattern of human life and the purposes of God. Our vision is only partial and often distorted, and this no doubt is the reason for much of our bewilderment and anguish of mind. If we could see the whole picture from God's angle, our bewilderment and anguish would be greatly lessened.

The Grace of God

A fourth alleviating factor is the manner in which so often the grace of God brings good out of evil and blessing out of trouble.

Let us look again at the Persian carpet in the making. Inevitably it happens that mistakes are made. Inattention, it may be, or carelessness or even willfulness, intrudes and an instruction is misheard or clumsily executed. Something goes into the carpet that should not be there. There is a blob of color, perhaps, in the wrong place and it looks as if the design is ruined. But what happens?

The master does not usually make the boy take out what has been wrongly woven in. Instead, he adapts his design in order to weave the mistake into the pattern and, in the end, although not quite what was originally intended, the carpet is no less lovely than it would have been.

In a similar way, given our cooperation, God can transform our mistakes and our accidents. He can make even our suffering a means of blessing and enrichment.

He does this on a broad scale. For instance, out of the horrible cataclysm and ghastly suffering of war He brings new discoveries in the art of healing that might well have lain hidden through many more years of peace. Out of the disaster of the great fire of London He brings better living conditions for the inhabitants of the future new city. Out of every air crash tragedy He brings increased safeguards for the future. Out of every situation of disaster and suffering some good result may be obtained.

This holds for individual experience, too.

We might refer to David Livingstone, his heart set on going as a medical missionary to China, broken-hearted when his ambition was denied him, and yet, as a result of this closed door, becoming the instrument to open up "darkest Africa" to the light of the Gospel. We might refer to Father Damien, who gave his life to work among the lepers. One day some boiling water was spilled on his foot and he felt no pain. "I am a leper," he thought in horror, and so he was. But what appeared at first utter disaster was turned to blessing. His ministry to the lepers became closer and more valuable, and his joy in serving them all the richer.

In Ralph Connor's little novel, *The Sky Pilot,* the prairie girl, Gwen, has a serious riding accident and is badly injured. The doctor's verdict is grave. She will probably never walk again, let alone ride. Gwen's reaction is one of angry resentment and rebellion. Bitterly she turns upon God and denounces His cruelty. It is then that the Sky Pilot, the itinerant preacher, tells her this parable.

Once upon a time there was a strong, young, healthy prairie that exulted in the wind and the sun. But one day a severe storm broke over the prairie and the lightning struck a severe blow right at the prairie's heart. For many a day the prairie was numbed and joyless and all who knew her mourned and wept. Then it was observed that a miracle had occurred. In the deep canyon cleft by the lightning stroke a carpet of pretty flowers was growing— gentle fragile flowers like violet and columbine that could never have survived on the open face of the prairie but were able to thrive in the shelter of the prairie's wound.

Out of even the worst disaster some good may be brought.

> One adequate support
> For the calamities of mortal life
> Exists, one only, an assured belief
> That the procession of our fate, howe'er
> Sad or disturbed, is ordered by a Being
> Of infinite benevolence and power,
> Whose everlasting purposes embrace
> All accidents, converting them to good.[3]

These are factors which may ease the anguish of mind that often comes from attempting to reconcile the fact of suffering with the love of an omnipotent God. All the same the problem of suffering remains. And the major part of that problem is not why it occurs but how it is to be faced.

John Ruskin says in *The Guests of God:*
Still from a thousand Calvarys the old cry goes up . . .
"My God, my God, why—?" Why do little children suf-

fer? Why is innocence made to bear the burden of the guilty? Why is all our life so "dark with grief and graves"? There are, of course, many ways in which we may seek to blunt the sharp edge of the problem. We may remind ourselves of what the world might have been if sin had not entered in to mar the divine purpose concerning it; we may call to mind how much of what is best in life we owe to the shaping hands of pain and sorrow; we may bring in another world to redress the balance of this, and say that the Divine Love has eternity to work in; above all, perhaps, we may take to heart Butler's great and always needed reminder of our ignorance and of our unfitness to judge the ways of God. Nevertheless . . .

As we close this chapter, we also are left with a "nevertheless," the nevertheless of the continuing fact of suffering, which neither the soundest nor the most plausible theory diminishes one whit. It is a fact which enters into the experience of us all, sometimes sooner, sometimes later, sometimes more, sometimes less. How are we to face it when it comes? Shall we conquer it or it conquer us?

NOTES

1. C. S. Lewis, *The Problem of Pain*, p. 132.
2. H. Wheeler Robinson, *Suffering, Human and Divine*, p. 39.
3. Wordsworth, *The Excursion*.

· 7 ·

Loving God

IN MANY CASES nothing helps more to relieve our anguish than to be assured that God loves us, and continues to love us even in our suffering. The authority for this assurance is found in Jesus.

It is not easier today to believe in God's love than it used to be. By no means. Many find it extremely difficult to believe that God loves them at any time, let alone when they are undergoing some experience of suffering.

Many, indeed, find it impossible to believe in God at all in this modern age. Horizons have widened so vastly and so rapidly that they feel God has been left behind in the speed of man's scientific advance. They listen to the Russian cosmonaut declaring, after returning from his flight in space, that he was able to detect no trace of God up there; and they conclude, along with him, that God does not exist.

A number of fallacies attend this conclusion but it is not our business to discuss them. All we say is that the Christian believes that God does exist and believes also that He cares for him, even in his suffering.

Jesus assures us that God cares for us individually. The whole character of His teaching bears this out and on several occasions He makes it quite explicit. One vivid example is His remark about the price of sparrows. "Look at the sparrows," He said, "How numerous they are. How small they are. How cheap they are—why, you can buy two for a penny and if you buy two pennyworths you get a fifth one thrown in for nothing. Yet God is aware of the existence even of each one of these sparrows. And you matter more to Him than many sparrows."(cf. Matt. 10:29 and Luke 12:6–7)

The death of Jesus confirms God's love for us and shows the lengths to which it is prepared to go.

Very likely no single factor is able to do more to encourage the sufferer than the knowledge that God allowed His own Son to suffer so much for the sake of mankind. For this means that, no matter how far out into the lonely wastes of personal suffering a man may have been driven, he is never on his own. Jesus has gone before him and is with him now.

> Father, if He, the Christ, were Thy revealer,
> Truly the first begotten of the Lord,
> Then Thou must be a Sufferer and a Healer—
> Pierced to the heart by the sorrow of Sword.
> Then must it mean, not only that Thy sorrow
> Smote Thee that once upon the lonely tree,
> But that today, tonight, and on the morrow,
> Still it will come. . . . O God, to Thee.

With lines like these Studdert Kennedy answered his own plaintive cry, "Are there no tears in the heart of the Eternal?"

Belief in God's participation in human suffering made a great difference, for example, to Michael Fairless, author of "The Roadmender." She was ill most of her life, and rarely free from pain; and the courage and serenity she showed in face of her adversity came in no small measure from her confidence that God had suffered on man's behalf and that God was sharing in her suffering now.

A biographical sketch of her says, "Across the whole world there lay for her the light of the glory of Divine Sacrifice. Not for her was any picture of a serene and far away God, without 'parts or passions,' looking on at the world's pain. It was the glory of her God to share all pain. There was no weariness of hers or any man's, no suffering that was not his."

George Eliot describes how Romola fled from Florence because life had become so difficult there that she felt she could no longer endure it. As she hurried away in tears she met Savonarola, who urged her to go back. "But," she protested, "I simply cannot bear it any longer." "My daughter," he replied, "you carry something within your mantle. Take it out and look at it." She took out the crucifix she carried with her and looked long at the figure of Jesus suffering on the cross. Thus reminded that in her suffering God was with her, she went back.

The knowledge that God was with him in his suffering has made a tremendous difference to many a sufferer. It may well do so to many another.

For one thing, it may ease that terrible agony of loneliness which is often his lot. Many sufferers find the hardest burden to bear is the feeling of separation which suffering brings with it. They feel cut off from their fellows and thrust out into a desolate place of solitude. The knowledge that God stands beside them in that desolate place goes a long way to make it more bearable.

For another thing, the fact that Jesus knew personally the solitude of suffering is a help. When, for example, a man is enduring severe pain he may feel desperately lonely. It can be a real solace to realize that Jesus also knew the loneliness of suffering and pain.

Alongside this stands the fact that the sufferings of Jesus were real and no mere make-believe. The pain Jesus felt was real pain. And it was intense and agonizing. Crucifixion was one of the most cruel and most painful modes of execution that man ever devised.

It is easy to overlook this. We view the Cross from the other side of Easter and may, therefore, fail to realize just what a terrible experience it was for Jesus.

Easter transformed Calvary. The final chapter of the story was one of glorious victory with the grave empty and Jesus risen. But this does not alter the awful fact of what the Cross meant to Jesus. Cross and Resurrection together present us with the Gospel, the Good News, and this may obscure to us the horror of the crucifixion. But on that first Good Friday it stood by itself and it was awful.

Even before Jesus was taken out to die He had already been "scourged." That is to say, He had been beaten with a several-thonged whip to whose leather thongs had been fixed pieces of sharpened bone and metal which had the effect of tearing flesh from the victim's back at every impact. This form of punishment was so severe that many men failed to survive it and many others went mad under it.

This, however, was only the prelude. After the scourging, in company with two criminals destined for a similar fate, He was led away to be crucified.

A Roman cross consisted of two parts—the upright beam which would already be at the place of execution and the cross beam which the victim himself was expected to carry. Jesus was, in fact, able to carry this only part of the way before physical weakness, no doubt through loss of blood and prolonged strain, caused Him to sink to His knees beneath its weight. It had to be carried the rest of the way by a pilgrim who happened at that moment to be passing by, Simon of Cyrene.

When they eventually arrived at the place of execution, Jesus was laid on the ground, the cross beam was thrust beneath his shoulders, his arms were stretched out on either side along its length, and nails were driven through his hands into the wood. The cross beam was then lifted up into position and fixed securely to the upright beam already standing in its prepared socket in the ground. What indescribable agony this must have caused.

The upright had a projecting ledge of wood, which acted as a kind of saddle, on which Jesus sat in order to lessen the strain on His hands, which otherwise would have been quickly torn away from the nails. His feet were fastened to the lower part of the upright, perhaps by cords, perhaps also by nails. Then He was left to hang in the mounting heat of the day for death to creep up on him slowly and painfully.

The agony of crucifixion has been described as the worst kind of agony. The unnatural position of the body and its effect on circulation, added to the damage inflicted on nerves and tendons by the driving of the nails through the hands, caused an intensity of suffering which grew worse with the passage of time. And this was aggravated by the severe thirst which in that climate swiftly assailed the crucified man as he hung unprotected from the heat.

Jesus, therefore, was well aware from personal experience what it was to suffer pain. But His suffering on Calvary was not limited to what it cost Him in terms of physical pain. The agony of mind and spirit He endured were equally intense. History has never heard another cry that plumbed the depths of such agony like the cry of Jesus from the Cross, "My God, my God, why hast thou forsaken me?"

All this is the measure of God's love for every one of us.

· 8 ·

Some Attitudes to the Problem

EVEN IF WE could explain suffering to our complete satisfaction, we would still have it to endure—and that is where its chief problem comes in. Before we speak about the attitude of Christian faith, which is, I believe, the best answer to it, we note some other attitudes that are adopted to suffering.

Suffering Is an Illusion

There is the attitude which insists that suffering is an illusion. Pain has no real existence, it is said. It exists only in the mind. Because of our limited understanding we attribute to it a reality which it does not possess.

This attitude has been argued by several systems of thought and more than one distinguished figure has been its protagonist. It is the outlook, for instance, of Christian Science and also of Hindu Vedantism. And there is food in it for profitable thought.

Suffering and the mind are, in fact, closely linked together and it cannot reasonably be denied that the degree of pain one feels frequently depends to a remarkable extent on one's mental approach to it. The counsel given by this philosophy, that we should tell ourselves that we are not really suffering, has some substance. A pessimistic outlook on one's suffering is likely to increase its pain, an optimistic one likely to reduce it.

At the same time, it is quite unrealistic to maintain that suffering is no more than an illusion of the mind. This famous limerick is not irrelevant here:

There was a faith healer of Deal
Who said "Although pain isn't real,
When I sit on a pin,
And it punctures my skin,
I dislike what I fancy I feel."

It is true that more and more unsuspected connections are being discovered between mind and matter. It is true that by strength of mind we can lessen, on occasion even eliminate, the feeling of physical pain in a given situation. Nonetheless, we do not remove all suffering merely by declaring that it does not exist. Grim realities like cancer, disseminated sclerosis, muscular dystrophy, and sudden bereavement, tend to be just as grim and just as real even if we say over and over again that they do not exist.

In Robert Bloch's novel *Psycho,* Norman Bates absolutely refuses to accept the fact of his mother's death. Plundering her grave, he takes away her body, practices his taxidermy on it, and proceeds to live as if the stuffed figure who shares his house is still alive. He goes on like this for years, living with a corpse that he refuses to accept as dead. It is a situation of great horror but its most tragic feature is not his horrifying relationship with a corpse but his delusion that the corpse is a living person.

He is shutting his eyes to the fact of death. But that does not alter the fact. His mother is still unable to speak to him. His refusal to admit that he is bereft does not restore her to life. It is true that in this way he does not feel the pain so acutely, but she is dead still and his loss just as great.

It is similarly true that we may often lessen a feeling of pain by playing it down in our minds, just as we may intensify it by building it up in our minds. But we do not remove it. And in some circumstances this is a stratagem that will have no effect. Man's suffering is no illusion. It is only too real.

Indifference

An attitude which has close affinities with the one we have been discussing is that which is counseled, for example, by Buddhism. It is the cultivation of a complete indifference to life and to the things of life. Suffering, it is said, is occasioned by desire, by concern over the things of the world and desire for them. Eliminate your interest in life and you will eliminate your suffering.

It is difficult to see quite how this is supposed to work with regard to actual physical pain. No matter how well one may cultivate an attitude of indifference to life, physical pain surely will still hurt. It would, however, be less than fair to leave the matter there. For Buddhism points forward rather to an *ultimate* freedom from pain through the achievement of total indifference.

Suffering is bound up with existence. Therefore the only way to cease from suffering is to cease to exist. Ordinarily—because an axiom of the Buddhist philosophy is the doctrine of continuous reincarnation—one passes from one life to another and so from one experience of suffering to another. It is, however, the desire to participate in life and its affairs that perpetuates this process of reincarnation. If one can achieve total indifference to life, then one may escape from the ceaseless round of birth and rebirth, into the state of Nirvana, the ideal state of complete disinterest and nonparticipation.

Even if it were possible, however, this would not be to conquer suffering. This is to be defeated by it, just as much as that man is defeated who seeks to escape from life's woes along the path of suicide.

The underlying philosophy of the Buddhist attitude has been adopted in varying degrees by some who do not otherwise subscribe to Buddhism. They reckon that the way to avoid hurt is to avoid becoming too much involved in life and in the affairs of life; and again it must be admitted that there is some truth here. Such an attitude will not, of course, take away physical pain. It may well, however, diminish considerably the amount of mental anguish and agony of spirit that would otherwise be experienced. The degree of mental and spiritual suffering that a man may sustain from any particular source is always in direct proportion to the degree of his involvement. The more a man loves a woman, for instance, the more he suffers when he loses her.

This is undoubtedly true. But is "contracting out" worthwhile? Is the decreased possibility of heartbreak a sufficient recompense for the decreased possibility of joy? For this also comes into the picture. The more a man loves a woman, the greater his joy to win her.

The noninvolvement method of combating suffering is to cultivate indifference and avoid becoming concerned about anything. But is not this also a kind of suicide? The withdrawal from heartbreak that it counsels can be achieved only through withdrawal from life. It is like a man seeking to be free from the pain of his corns by cutting off his feet. There is no doubt that such a desperate expedient will remove his corns. But does it not make his situation a great deal worse?

Even if complete withdrawal could be achieved it would be tantamount to ceasing to live. Is it worth it, even if it means the avoidance of suffering? Here is a man, say, who has lost his mental grip and lives in a vacuum of indifference. It is true that most of the heartbreak and anguish of life passes him by. But which of us would envy him for that, when we remember the price he pays?

If we cultivate an attitude of indifference to life in general, and to its various activities and relationships, we may well fashion for ourselves a shield that will protect us, in some degree at least, from the probing lance of suffering. But the cost is to be measured in terms of the sacrifice of a great deal of our personality and of our intended destiny. It is better surely to be a man, even a man in the grip of suffering, than to be a cow placidly content in the field or a vegetable unfeelingly sunning itself in the garden.

Resignation

Another attitude is resignation. This says, "Well, it has got to be. Therefore we must just put up with it." It is an attitude which makes its appearance in different camps. It is the attitude of the fatalist who says, "Whatever is to be will be." It is the attitude of the Moslem who says, "It is the will of Allah." It is the attitude—strangely, for it is not truly a Christian attitude—of some Christians, who say, "It is God's will."

This attitude may produce patience in face of suffering and can be helpful. But it can be harmful. It has often, for instance, been the enemy of progress, an impediment to man's attempt to improve his own lot and that of his fellow. It has often meant the acceptance of conditions which, far from being a "must be," could have been changed for the better.

One of Stanley Jones's stories is of a Swami talking to a rich landowner in India and urging him to make conditions easier and happier for his tenants. To every point that was raised the landowner simply said, "It is the will of God for them." At last the Swami lost patience, pulled off his shoe, and struck the landowner over the back—a deadly insult—and shouted, "Then this is the will of God for you."

In any case, while the attitude of resigned submission may encourage patience in the experience of suffering, it falls far short of being a real answer to the problem. For it leaves suffering still the master.

The Resolve Not to Surrender

Nor is suffering defeated by the stoical attitude which some adopt as their defense. This attitude is determined—at whatever cost—not to bow the knee. It is determined not to weep or flinch or betray any sign of being wounded. It meets every suffering with teeth tightly clenched and a grim resolve not to surrender.

It is the attitude of these lines:

Though I am beaten
Nobody shall know.
I'll wear defeat proudly.
I shall go
About my business
As I did before.
Only when I have safely
Closed the door
Against friends and the rest
Shall I be free
To bow my head
Where there is none to see.

Tonight I will shed my tears.
Tomorrow when
I talk with you
I will be gay again.
Though I am beaten
Nobody shall guess,
For I will walk
As though I knew success.

There is a quality of courage in this that demands respect. But it is not a way of victory. It is an acceptance of defeat. It aims no higher than to be a gallant loser. The Christian Gospel offers a better answer than this.

Rebellion and Bitterness

There is another attitude to be mentioned. It is in no sense an answer to the problem of suffering. But it is the response that many make to suffering in their own lives, the response of resentment and rebellion, anger and bitterness.

In this attitude several elements may be combined. There is often a bewailing of one's luck. "How singularly unfortunate I am," the sufferer laments. "Why should this have come upon *me*, while so-and-so next door is entirely free from trouble?" And so he enfolds himself in a cocoon of self-pity which has no effect except to make his situation less bearable than ever.

There is often a blaming of it all on God. "God has done this and He has been most unfair," is the cry. "He should have ordered things much better and certainly should have prevented this happening to *me*."

With this often goes a rebellion of spirit against God and sometimes even an abandoning of faith. Thinking that his faith has let him down, the sufferer turns his back on God.

A woman I knew reacted like this. She and her sister were very close. One day her sister died suddenly and nothing I could say was able to get through to her. She was polite and courteous to me but implacably sullen toward God. He had treated her very badly. He had cruelly taken away the sister she needed so much and would miss so terribly. Persistently she rebuffed my every effort to suggest that comfort and healing might be found in Christ. Determinedly she remained immersed in her deep pool of self-pity, forswearing Church and Gospel.

There is no answer to the problem of suffering in this. Indeed, no attitude could be less helpful. The reaction of resentful rebellion achieves nothing except to aggravate the distress of our situation and to make our ultimate defeat more sure. The only real answer to suffering—and the only real hope of victory—lies in the Christian Gospel.

· 9 ·

The Christian Attitude

THE REAL PROBLEM of suffering is not the why but the how of it, not the finding of a satisfactory explanation but the finding of the means to meet it without being crushed. I believe that the Christian Gospel provides the means of victory. Jesus has not explained human suffering. But, more important, He has overcome it and, through faith in Him, we may overcome it, too.

Even if a full explanation of suffering were available its real problem would persist.

Here, say, is a man lying in a hospital bed. He has been involved in a serious car accident and badly injured. It so happens that he knows exactly why the accident occurred. He is aware of all the various factors that contributed to the actual collision and understands with perfect clarity the reason for his lying smashed up in that bed. But his understanding of the circumstances is of little help in meeting his adversity.

Here, say, is a sailor caught in a storm at sea. He knows exactly, let us suppose, how the currents and the winds and all the relevant weather factors have combined to produce the tempest. But that knowledge will not be enough to enable him to ride out the storm successfully.

Our situation is not greatly dissimilar. We are all, as it were, making a voyage upon the ocean of life. In the course of that voyage we encounter storms, sometimes greater, sometimes less. We may wrestle as we will with the problem of their origin but, no matter how well we come to understand them, we need something more to ride them out successfully. It is this "something more" that the Gospel of Christ makes available.

Jesus does not help us combat suffering by screening us from it. Christian faith does not deliver a man from experience of suffering. Sometimes, in fact, his faith may bring him a deeper experience of suffering than would otherwise have been his.

It is well to be quite clear about this, for the idea persists that the man of faith will be spared suffering because of his faith. A text like Psalm 119:117 is quoted ("Hold me up, that I may be safe"), or a passage like "Because you have made the Lord your refuge . . . no evil shall befall you" (Psalm 91:9–10) is referred to and the idea is fostered that Christian belief will ensure physical safety.

During time of war, for instance, some seek of refuge in this conviction. But it is plainly not the case that God preserves the believer from physical ill. Bombs, for example, kill and maim Christians as well as non-Christians. This does not mean that Psalm 119:117 is a lie. It means, however, that its essential truth is rather different from that understanding of it. The believer, *no matter what disaster may overtake him,* is still safe, for he is in God's safekeeping.

This is what Jesus made clear. This is the kind of safety that He promised to His followers. He never at any time promised that, if a man were to follow Him, suffering would pass him by or be reduced. On the contrary, Jesus took care to make it plain that those who should follow Him continued to be wayfarers in this world and as such would meet suffering. "In the world," He affirmed to His followers, "you have tribulation."

But He goes on to affirm, "But be of good cheer, I have overcome the world." (John 16:33) He promises, not freedom from the worst, but "safety" in spite of it.

And He keeps His word. If we are Christ's, we remain His in disaster and are still His even in death. Catastrophe may kill us but it cannot destroy us. As was once said of the Christian's outlook, "We do not know what the future holds, but we know who holds the future."

Those who lived through World War II in Britain may remember how, at one stage, night after night the BBC news would speak of Royal Air Force raids over enemy territory. Always the bulletin would end with a statement like this: "All of our pilots are safe," or "Two of our pilots are missing," or "Three of our aircraft failed to return."

One day an obituary notice appeared in one of the daily papers. It told briefly and simply of the death in action of an RAF flyer and the notice ended with the words, "One of our pilots is safe."

What matters most is not what happens to us in our journey through life, nor how well we understand what is happening to us at any given time. What matters most is our reaction to what happens. The claim of the Gospel is that by Christ's help we may be "more than conquerors" whatever befalls us. It declares that every experience of suffering may be transformed by the power of God made readily available in Jesus Christ.

John Ruskin was once in the company of a lady who dropped a blot of ink on her beautiful silk handkerchief. "Oh," she cried in great dismay, "my lovely handkerchief is ruined." "Perhaps not," said Ruskin, "please leave it with me."

A little later he returned her handkerchief, but it was no longer disfigured. Unable to remove the blot, Ruskin had used it as a basis for a most attractive design. The handkerchief, far from being ruined, was now even lovelier than it had been.

It is the making possible of a transformation of this nature that is the Gospel's answer to the problem of suffering, a transformation of even the most unsightly blots that may happen along to disfigure our lives. This is what Jesus did with the suffering that came His own way. He accepted it without bitterness or rancor and transformed it.

This is supremely illustrated in the Cross. No greater tragedy could be imagined than this, no fate more undeserved, no suffering more agonizing. Yet out of it Jesus brought good. He took all the suffering and evil that was Calvary and out of it He fashioned the greatest victory that history has ever seen—and the most important.

The victory of Easter was a victory won over all the forces of sin and suffering and death. And it was not won simply by Jesus for Jesus. It was won by Him for us all.

The great Easter victory is one which we may share. This is what the Gospel has to say in face of suffering. If we are Christ's, suffering may still come our way; but in His keeping we are safe and secure, even though we should lose everything in the world, even though we should lose life itself.

> In pastures green? Not always: sometimes He
> Who knoweth best, in kindness leadeth me
> By weary ways, where heavy shadows be.
> And by still waters? No, not always so:
> Oft-times the heavy tempests round me blow,
> And o'er my soul the waves and billows go.
> But when the storm is loudest, and I cry
> Aloud for help, the Master standeth by,
> And whispers to my soul, "Lo, it is I."
> Above the tempest wild I hear Him say,
> "Beyond the darkness lies the perfect day,
> In every path of thine I lead the way."

So, whether on the hill-tops high and fair
I dwell, or in the sunless valleys where
The shadows lie—what matters? He is there.

Do what we like and take what evasive action we may, suffering of some kind is bound to overtake us in the end. But the Gospel declares that it can be overcome. This is not just pious platitude, it is sober truth. Tens of thousands of lives down the centuries bear witness to it and many of us have personal knowledge of such witness.

Rita Snowden speaks of seeing a wonderful old face that was "full of suffering, full also of the overcoming of it." One of my own precious memories is of shaking hands with the famous Japanese Christian, Toyohiko Kagawa. *His* was a face that was "full of suffering, full also of the overcoming of it." Few men have endured so much suffering as he. But it never took the smile from his face. He had found the secret of conquering it.

Von Hügel is right when he says that Christianity does not explain suffering but shows us what to do with it. Many things may befall the Christian which will puzzle and perplex him. But nothing can befall him which need finally defeat him. Jesus can make him victor even over the worst.

This, then, is the Christian answer to the problem of suffering. Not that it may be explained. Not that it may be avoided. But that it may be overcome.

Stanley Jones tells how in India the "brain-fever bird" cries out unceasingly in the hot days, "Brain-fever, brain-fever, brain-fever," and how its shrill notes were driving him to the point of despair, when suddenly he found the way to defeat it. He realized its notes could also be made to read, "Hallelujah, hallelujah, hallelujah." From then on it troubled him no more.

The affirmation of the Christian Gospel may be expressed in similar terms. When life calls out insistently in some dark and painful circumstance, "Brain-fever, brain-fever, brain-fever," we may have these notes of torture transformed through Christ into a triumphant series of hallelujahs. This is what is meant when the Scripture says, "All things work together for good to them that love God." (Romans 8:28) No matter what may happen, Christian faith can capture it for God so that in the end something good may be brought out of it.

This is surely what Percy Ainsworth had in mind when he wrote his sonnet about roses:

> My garden has roses red,
> My garden has roses white,
> But if when the day is sped
> I stand by the gate at night,
> One fragrance comes, when the day is dead,
> From my roses white and my roses red.
> The roses of joy are red,
> The roses of pain are white;
> But I think, when the day is sped
> And I stand by the gate at night,
> I shall know just this, when the day is dead,
> That a rose is sweet, be it white or red.[1]

Christ can give us the victory over suffering if we are prepared to accept it from him, if—as Stanley Jones might put it—we are willing to have our wings set the victory way. "When a storm strikes an eagle, he sets his wings in such a way that the air currents send him above the storm by their very fury. The set of the wings does it. The Christian is not spared the pains and sorrows and sicknesses that come upon other people, but he is given an inner set of spirit by which he rises above these calamities."[2]

This is more than mere pious cant. This is not just like Don Quixote's cardboard visor—something that may be regarded as a protection only so long as it is not put to the test. This is something that works. Those many thousands of men and women who have experienced the Christian victory over suffering are the evidence that it does.

Suffering will still come the way of Christians and sometimes it may be severe. But, however severe it is, Jesus can help them through. A bird sitting on a tree in a gale may be dislodged from its perch by the force of the wind. This will be a most frightening and uncomfortable experience. But it is not—or need not be, at any rate—final disaster. For it still has its wings.

Often Christians may be badly buffeted by life's storms. But they, too, have wings, the wings of their faith.

There is a single word in the Authorized Version rendering of the Book of Acts which may be taken as both symbol and summary of our thesis.

With the martyrdom of Stephen, the dam of restraint was finally breached and the piled up waters of fear and hate swept forth across the infant Jerusalem Church and threatened to destroy it utterly. For a time, although the authorities had been uneasily hostile, counsels of restraint had prevailed and there had been little open persecution of the new Christian sect. This gave the newborn Church a chance to grow and expand. Then came the murder of Stephen, and such violent persecution of the Christians followed that most of them were forced to flee the city.

As a result, the Jerusalem Church that had been thriving so well was almost wiped out. It was a disaster—but it was not allowed to be final disaster. Because of the continuing faith of those upon whom the calamity fell, great good emerged from it and the Church, far from being destroyed, spread all the further and all the faster. It was, in the end, as if a wood fire had been kicked apart and the scattered burning brands started other fires to produce a greater conflagration than ever.

"At that time there was a great persecution against the Church which was at Jerusalem; and they were all scattered abroad throughout the regions of Judea and Samaria, except the apostles. . . . *Therefore* they that were scattered abroad went everywhere preaching the word" (Acts 8:1, 4).

The key word is *therefore*. Tragedy had struck and the Christians were driven where they had no desire to be, to their great regret and bitter heartbreak. But they held to their faith in the unwanted situation into which they found themselves thrust, and as a result their calamity was overmastered to a good end.

Whenever people make that "therefore" their own in time of suffering, victory will be theirs. If, like these early Christians, they hold to their faith even in the darkness, they shall be more than conquerors through Jesus Christ.

This is the Christian answer.

NOTES

1. Percy Ainsworth, *Roses,* Poems and Sonnets.
2. S. Jones, *Christ and Human Suffering,* p. 99.

Even in Bereavement

BEREAVEMENT is the most universal of man's experience of suffering and also one of the most heartbreaking. But Christian faith can give a great deal of help even here; and there can be a vast difference between the Christian and the non-Christian in a time of bereavement.

This is not to say that the Christian feels the parting less. It is not that for him the loss of the loved one is less painful. Often it is the other way round. But for the Christian other factors enter in which, though they do not remove his grief, overmaster it.

There is, for one, the conviction that a Christian never really dies but, in the experience that men call death, simply passes from one kind of life to another.

The Christian believes that the Savior who rose from the grave and appeared alive on Easter Day conquered death not only in that particular instance and for himself but conquered it eternally and for any and all willing to avail themselves of the victory offered. The Gospel declares that for the man in Christ death is not the end but a new beginning.

Canon Dick Sheppard ministered at St. Martin-in-the-Fields in London between the wars. When he died, as he did quite suddenly, one of the morning papers printed a large photograph of his pulpit at St. Martin's. There it was, just the same as ever, but empty, and on the reading desk the Bible lay open with a shaft of light striking full across it. And beneath the picture were the words, "Here endeth the first lesson."

Moreover, believing that death is the transition to new life, bereaved Christians are confident that their loved ones are not lost to them forever. In a real sense and in a heartrending sense, they *are* lost. They are gone from sight and no longer occupy the familiar places they once did in the lives of their friends. But there is the prospect of reunion with them in Heaven. The separation caused by death, though full of pain, is temporary.

More than that, the Christian believes that the separation of death is not complete even now. The Creed affirms, "I believe in the Communion of Saints." That is not just an empty phrase. It declares that there is a fellowship of Christian people ("Saints") everywhere, both in Heaven and upon earth. If that is true, then the ties which bind us to our Christian friends are not fully severed, even temporarily, by the hand of death. We are still linked to them even when death divides us.

In fact, they are not so far away as we may often imagine. In a fashion, it is as if they were in the next room, separated from us but still very near.

> No, not cold beneath the grasses,
> Not close-walled within the tomb;
> Rather in my Father's mansion,
> Living in another room.
> Living, like the one who loves me,
> Like yon child with cheeks abloom,
> Out of sight, at desk or school book,
> Busy in another room.
> Nearer than the youth whom fortune
> Beckons where the strange lands loom;
> Just behind the hanging curtain,
> Serving in another room.
> Shall I doubt my Father's mercy,
> Shall I think of death as doom.
> Or the stepping o'er the threshold
> To a bigger, brighter room?

It is an enormous help to be assured that our dead Christian friends are really alive still and that they are not lost to us for ever, perhaps not completely lost to us even now. It helps, too, to have the assurance that theirs has been a change for the better, not the worse.

D. L. Moody once said to a group of friends, "One day you will pick up your newspaper and read that D. L. Moody is dead. When you do, don't believe it. At that moment I shall be more alive than I am now."

Death for the Christian is not loss but gain. This is our faith.

Shall I wear mourning for my soldier dead,
I—a believer? Give me red.
Or give me royal purple for the king
At whose high court my love is visiting.
Dress me in green for growth, for life made new.
For skies his dear feet march, dress me in blue,
In white for his white soul; robe me in gold
For all the pride that his new rank shall hold.
In earth's dim gardens blooms no hue too bright
To dress me for my love who walks in light.

Some years ago a much loved friend of mine decided to emigrate. When the time came for him to go, it was a sad occasion for us both. The night before he left he came up to my manse and we sat and talked for a long time, jealous of these last minutes together and reluctant to bring them to a close. But at last he could wait no longer and our goodbyes had to be said. I can see him still as he left me. The beauty of the May evening seemed only to enhance the sadness that I felt as he walked away, came to the bend in the road, turned and waved, and passed out of sight.

I have not seen him since and I do not know whether I shall ever see him again. I missed him a great deal then and I miss him still. But for him the change was much more of gain than of loss, and I do not grudge him it. He has prospered in his adopted land and is very happy.

Nor is he completely lost to me. Although half the world divides us, letters keep us in touch and a real fellowship still survives. And I believe that, whether or not I see him again in this life, I shall meet him again in our Father's House.

This experience resembles what it is when death steps between Christian people. Those who take leave of us in death gain rather than lose by the change: They are not completely lost to us even now; and we may look forward confidently to reunion with them when we in turn move on from this life.

· 11 ·
Twenty Years On

IT IS NOW twenty years since 1969, when I wrote this book. These years have witnessed many changes in the world and in society, some of them cataclysmic. During this period, for instance, the dreadful scourge of AIDS has appeared on our horizon to darken it with sorrow and with dread. What corresponding changes, you may wonder, have these years and my experiences in them occasioned with regard to the thoughts expressed in this book twenty years ago?

The simple answer is, "Little or none"—otherwise I would not be letting the book go out again practically untouched except for this new chapter. Rather, my additional twenty years' experience has confirmed me in such understanding as I have of the answers the Christian faith has to offer to the incessant and universal questions concerning human suffering.

I have received further confirmation in this respect by the large number of expressions of thanks sent to me by those who have been helped through reading my book. These have come to me from many quarters and from not a few situations of extreme distress of one kind or another.

This has persuaded me to have my book issued afresh much as it was, in the hope and with the prayer that it may be a means of help to many more people as they grapple with the problem of suffering.

During the past twenty years much has been added to the world's tally of suffering. A multitude of disasters have occurred, a great many of which have been of national or even international proportions. I am thinking of such calamities as Chernobyl, Armenia, Piper Alpha, Lockerbie, Hillsborough. These have caused such suffering and pain and heartbreak as were almost impossible to contemplate; and with them age-old cries were raised again from many sides.

"Why does God do such things?" It is no less important now than it was twenty years ago to protest, against the background of such massive disasters, that God does *not* do these things. He does not sit at his desk in some great celestial office and decree that such-and-such a catastrophe will happen in such-and-such a location at such-and-such a time. These disasters are the consequence not of God's deliberate dictate but of human action, or natural cause and effect, or a combination of the two.

"Why does God not prevent the occurrence of such things?" It still needs to be pointed out that for God to make a practice of intervening to avert the consequences of man's folly or man's wickedness or the processes of nature's laws would be to turn the world topsy-turvy; and far from making human life more pleasant, it would make it much more difficult if not impossible.

"Why did God not make a world that was free from the possibility of disasters?" Ultimately, the answer to this question lies in the heart and mind of God. But it does seem to me still, as it seemed twenty years ago, that Jesus, the supreme revealer of God, has made it overwhelmingly plain that God is love and that, therefore, he would not, could not create a world for his beloved creation to inhabit that was less than what was best. Somehow, then, however difficult it sometimes is for our finite human understanding to comprehend fully, this world in which we live—the creation of a loving God—had to contain the risk of suffering and disaster. Apparently, this was because it had to enshrine freedom of choice for mankind with all the risks inherent in that, and also to enshrine a system of natural law and order that could at times lead to earthquake, flood or fire.

In the twenty years since I wrote this book I have been shocked and grieved, as have we all, at the many headline-demanding disasters. I have been grieved, too, by the explosion of the terrible modern plague of AIDS upon the human scene. But I refuse to explain it in terms of God exacting punishment for sin.

As Jesus makes it impossible to think of God as a capricious deity who indiscriminately ladles out with one hand a dollop of happiness to A and with the other hand a dollop of misery to B, so he makes it equally impossible to think of God as one who dispenses a quota of punishment in strict retaliation for any and every sin committed. That the occurrence of AIDS is closely linked with man's selfishness and foolishness and disregard of God's ways is beyond doubt. In that sense there is a real element of retribution involved. But it is what men have brought upon themselves, not what God has decreed should happen to them—a vastly different thing.

Suppose a parent out of love and concern warns his child that it is dangerous to play with fire and pleads with him never to do it; and suppose that child nevertheless plays with fire and is burned. There is a quality of inevitable retribution in that, but it is in no way a matter of parental punishment.

And sometimes when a child willfully persists in playing with fire other totally innocent parties may also be burned. Similarly, the scourge of AIDS can and does involve innocent parties. Any theory of divine retribution must surely founder on this rock, if on nothing else.

Over these past twenty years I have also been grieved, as a parish minister, by a multitude of personal disasters and sorrows.

During these years I have sat at the bedsides of hundreds of men and women and children who were ill or injured, and hundreds, too, who were dying.

I have attempted, as best I could, to counsel hundreds whose lives were in a mess for one reason or another.

I have conducted some 1,400 funeral services.

In circumstances such as these I have been personally involved, in greater or lesser degree, in situations of suffering and of heartbreak. Some of them were particularly heartrending, like the time when Carole Harper died.

I had enjoyed a long relationship of deep friendship with all the family. Her mother and father had been active and loyal members of my Youth Fellowship and later of my congregation. I had married them and baptized their children. Ken was now an elder and superintendent of the Sunday School, while Morag was in charge of the Brownie Guides. Carole was twenty-one years of age, a student at Glasgow Art School, and very talented as well as very lovely.

Early one never-to-be-forgotten morning, Morag telephoned me to say that Carole had died suddenly, overnight. The postmortem revealed that the cause was an asthma attack coupled with an unsuspected influenza virus.

That was one of the most harrowing and most demanding bereavement experiences I have ever had to face. But there was a great depth of sorrow and pain in hundreds of other cases, too, with which I had to deal.

In so many such circumstances and occasions I have heard again the agonized cries ascend, "Why? Why? Why?" And over and over again I have tried, to the best of my ability, to alleviate in some degree the agony of those who were making the cries. And I have tried to do so along the lines this book has followed. I have tried to persuade them that God is not the cause of their distress and that he has not chosen them to suffer in this way. In particular I have tried always to assure them that God still loves them and that far from sending their suffering upon them, he shares in it, suffering with them, just as he suffered with his Son on Calvary.

There used to be a painting hanging in Manchester Art Gallery which depicted Jesus on the Cross. At first sight the painting presented a very somber appearance. There was Jesus hanging on the cross, enshrouded in thick darkness. And to begin with that was all the beholder could see. But if one looked longer and more closely, one could detect through the darkness the arms of God enfolding and upholding his suffering and dying Son.

What this book is most of all concerned to say is that, whenever a disaster occurs, God is always in the midst of it and his arms of love are always there to enfold and uphold the sufferer if he or she will permit him.

The twenty years that have come and gone since I first wrote this book have made me more convinced that the most important question concerning our human suffering is not any of its "Whys" but its "How": How are we to face up and win through when it comes to our own door, as it always does sooner or later?

During these two decades the background and the scenery have often been vastly different, but the same basic dramas of suffering have kept being played out and the same questions have kept arising. Answers are no easier now than they were in 1969.

Bullets and bombs still wound and destroy the bodies of believers in God just as ruthlessly as they do the bodies of unbelievers.

Prayer is no more of an invincible shield against the onset of pain and sorrow now than it was then.

The innocent still suffer in their thousands, and sometimes still the guilty appear to get off lightly.

The good news is that, given the chance, the Christian faith still works. God still cares and Jesus is still able and willing to supply strength and comfort, and even victory. I have seen much additional suffering in these twenty years, but I have also seen much magnificent Christ-aided overcoming of it.

Ken and Morag Harper are one couple who spring to mind. Carole's death was a desperately heavy blow to them, and the funeral service, with the church packed to the door, must have been full of pain. But their Christian faith gave them the courage and the strength to go on and keep going on in a manner that was an inspiration to their minister and all their other friends. They, like St. Paul, became "more than conquerors through him that loved us."

One of the saddest occasions in which I have been personally involved since this book was written was when my brother's daughter, Sandra, had a very serious accident. Just short of her eighteenth birthday and training to be a nurse, she toppled three floors down into the stairwell of the Nurses Home at Glasgow Royal Infirmary. She sustained severe injuries that left her completely paralyzed from the waist down and with her left arm totally disabled.

It was a horrific accident and a horrific outcome. Most people in such a situation would, I fancy, have been embittered and resentful, full of "Whys" and "If onlys." Sandra rebuked, humbled, and uplifted us all by her attitude of acceptance and positive faith. "It has happened," she said. "It can't be undone. I must just make the best of things as they are with Jesus to help me." And she has, in a marvelous way. That was sixteen years ago. Her physical condition has not, and cannot, improve—but she has surely conquered it.

Not everyone reacts like this. Just last week I was speaking to a woman newly admitted to the little hospital where I serve as part-time chaplain. I found her uncompromisingly bitter in her condemnation of God. "I was a Sunday school teacher for thirty-five years," she told me. "I nursed my invalid husband for a number of years after that, with my own life consequently very restricted. Now my husband has died and I have suffered a stroke that has left me incapacitated. It's just terrible that after all my devoted service God should let this happen to me. And look at my son—he's an atheist, and yet life is treating him very well. I simply don't believe in God any longer."

In face of her tirade I could not help thinking wryly of the piece of wall graffiti I once saw which said, "Thank God I'm an atheist." But I was sorry for her and concerned. I quite failed, however, to soften her attitude. It is such a pity for she is making her adversity doubly hard to bear and shutting her door against the help Jesus could give her. I will keep trying and hoping, encouraged a bit by the fact that the embittered lady of whom I speak on page 65 returned to church and to faith after many years away.

I pray this lady may also do so in time, for I am in no doubt that Jesus Christ has the best and most helpful answer to the problem of any suffering that may come to us. Not that he will explain everything to us. That probably would not help a great deal anyway. But he will share our suffering with us and help us battle through it.

Prayers for Suffering People

For one who suffers constant pain

O GOD, help me to endure my pain with dignity
And prevent my faith from weakening under it.
I am aware that I am often irritable,
Especially when the pain is very bad.
Please forgive me
And give me grace
To be easier to live with
Despite my pain.
Help those who have to do with me
To be understanding and patient.
I find my pain difficult to bear,
Sometimes very difficult,
Particularly in the lonely reaches of the night.
Keep me mindful of your nearness
And let the thought of that be a help to me.
Keep me mindful of your sympathy
And let that be a help, too.
Keep me mindful of your power
And let me draw on that to see me through.
FOR JESUS' SAKE *Amen*

WE are afflicted in every way, but not crushed; perplexed, but not driven to despair; persecuted, but not forsaken; struck down, but not destroyed ... So we do not lose heart. Though our outer nature is wasting away, our inner nature is being renewed every day. For this slight momentary affliction is preparing for us an eternal weight of glory beyond all comparison, because we look not to the things that are seen but to the things that are unseen; for the things that are seen are transient, but the things that are unseen are eternal. For we know that if the earthly tent we live in is destroyed, we have a building from God, a house not made with hands, eternal in the heavens. (2 Corinthians 4:8–9, 16 and 5:1)

For one who is no longer able to work

O GOD, I feel so useless
And such a nuisance
And a drag on other people.
I used to be so strong and so able.
I used to find my work no trouble.
But now it is beyond me.
I dislike being idle.
I dislike being so dependent on others.
It irks me sorely that I cannot work.
And is discoloring my whole outlook.
Show me the wisdom of accepting what cannot be
    changed
With as good grace as possible
And of making the best of it.
Help me to make the best of my inability to work.
Help me to make full use of my increased
opportunities to do other things,
To talk and to listen, to read and to observe.
Help me to find unspoiled delight in the compan-
    ionship
Of those who love me

And who work for me as once I worked for others.
Help me to grip the strong hand of the Carpenter
of Nazareth
And from it to draw courage and comfort and
peace.
FOR JESUS' SAKE. *Amen*

I LIFT up my eyes to the hills. From whence does my help
come? My help comes from the Lord, who made heaven
and earth. He will not let your foot be moved, he who
keeps you will not slumber. Behold, he who keeps Israel
will neither slumber nor sleep. The Lord is your keeper;
the Lord is your shade on your right hand. The sun shall
not smite you by day, nor the moon by night. The Lord
will keep you from all evil; he will keep your life. The
Lord will keep your going out and your coming in from
this time forth and for evermore. (Psalm 121)

For one who is losing his sight

O GOD, I can no longer see very well,
Soon I shall be completely blind.
I cannot deny that I dread the thought of it.
To have to move around by touch instead of sight,
To be dependent on others for so many things,
To be deprived of the beauty of color,
To be denied the joy of seeing my loved ones'
faces—
The prospect fills me with dismay and with fear.
I could not stand it at all were it not for you.
But I know that you love me
And that you will never leave me.

I know, too, that I have a lot to be thankful for.
I have seen many lovely sights and they are stored
    in my memory.
I have good friends who will be of great assistance
    to me.
I have the example of others who have learned to
    adjust to blindness.
I have the light of the Gospel which no sightless-
    ness can hide.
Help me to face the future bravely
And to avoid the temptation of too much self-pity.
Help me to overcome discouragement and disap-
    pointment
And to adapt successfully to my new situation.
I know, Lord, that faith can give me the victory
    even here.
Please let me find it.
FOR JESUS' SAKE *Amen*

THE Lord is my shepherd, I shall not want; he makes me
lie down in green pastures. He leads me beside still waters;
he restores my soul. He leads me in paths of righteousness
for his name's sake. Even though I walk through the valley
of the shadow of death, I fear no evil; for thou art with
me; thy rod and thy staff, they comfort me. Thou prepar-
est a table before me in the presence of my enemies; thou
anointest my head with oil, my cup overflows. Surely
goodness and mercy shall follow me all the days of my life;
and I shall dwell in the house of the Lord for ever. (Psalm
23)

For one who is lonely

O GOD, I lead a very lonely life
And sometimes I am sick with misery because of
    it.
Few people call on me
And I can go for days without a conversation.
I have no real friends
And no one I can turn to with my troubles.
Perhaps the fault is mine,
Perhaps I do not invite friendship,
But I would like to have some in my life.
Help me to find it.
Help me, too, to remember that Jesus is my friend
And that He is with me always
And that He cares for me
And that He understands me.
Keep me mindful, that no matter how lonely I
    may otherwise be,
I can never be completely alone if I am His.
FOR JESUS' SAKE *Amen*

NOW the eleven disciples went to Galilee, to the mountain to which Jesus had directed them. And when they saw him they worshiped him; but some doubted. And Jesus came and said to them, "All authority in heaven and on earth has been given to me. Go therefore and make disciples of all nations, baptizing them in the name of the Father and of the Son and of the Holy Spirit, teaching them to observe all that I have commanded you; and lo, I am with you always, to the close of the age." (Matthew 28, 16–20)

For one who has lost a limb

O GOD, I need your help.
Please give it to me.
I am going to miss my limb very much.
In fact, I do not know how I am going to manage
    without it.
But I know it can be done.
Others have done it.
And I can do it too.
But I need your help.
I need to be able to adjust myself mentally,
I need to be strong spiritually,
Before I can tackle the physical problems in-
    volved.
But with you to help me I can succeed.
It will not be easy.
It will take effort and persistence.
There may be disappointments and frustrations.
But it can be done.
With your help it will be done.
Please help me all you can.
FOR JESUS' SAKE *Amen*

THEN Jesus made the disciples get into the boat and go
before him to the other side, while he dismissed the
crowds. And after he had dismissed the crowds, he went
up into the hills by himself to pray. When evening came,
he was there alone, but the boat by this time was many
furlongs distant from the land, beaten by the waves; for
the wind was against them. And in the fourth watch of the
night he came to them, walking on the sea. But when the

disciples saw him walking on the sea, they were terrified, saying, "It is a ghost!" And they cried out for fear. But immediately he spoke to them, saying, "Take heart, it is I; have no fear." (Matthew 14: 22–27)

For one who has lost his hearing

O GOD, how I wish I had appreciated more the
    gift of hearing.
For now that I have lost it
I miss it terribly.
How I wish I could hear again
The song of birds in the morning,
The lapping of waves on the shore,
The sighing of wind in the trees.
How I wish I could hear again
The sound of music,
The noise of traffic,
The speech of friends.
But I should not dwell on these things.
This is to encourage self-pity,
And makes matters worse.
Let me dwell instead, O Lord, on all those lovely
    sounds
That I have heard
And that I can hear again and again
In my memory whenever I wish.
Let me dwell especially on the Good News I have
    heard
That you are love
And that in you is life eternal.
May I remember that no deafness can ever shut
    out your voice

But only an unwillingness to hear.
Let me be willing, O Lord,
So that I shall not miss your words of comfort,
Nor your words of challenge.
FOR JESUS' SAKE *Amen*

FINALLY, brethren, whatever is true, whatever is honor-
able, whatever is just, whatever is pure, whatever is lovely,
whatever is gracious, if there is any excellence, if there is
anything worthy of praise, think about these things. What
you have learned and received and heard and seen in me,
do; and the God of peace will be with you ... I have
learned, in whatever state I am, to be content. I know how
to be abased, and I know how to abound; in any and all
circumstances I have learned the secret of facing plenty
and hunger, abundance and want. I can do all things in
him who strengthens me. (Philippians 4: 8–9, 11–13)

For one who is afraid of being ill

O GOD, you know how out of sorts I have been
     lately.
You know, too, how reluctant I am to see the doc-
     tor.
I am afraid of what he might say
And of what he might find.
I am afraid it may be something serious.
I am afraid I may have to go into hospital.
Help me to see that to be brave is to be wise.
Help me to have the courage to face up to this.
Let me realize
That if it is nothing serious
I am worrying needlessly.
Let me realize, too,
That if it is something serious

The sooner it is diagnosed the sooner it can be
    helped.
Let me realize most of all
That, whatever the position may be,
Your love is with me now and will be with me
    always.
Give me the peace of mind
And strength of spirit
Which should come from knowing this.
FOR JESUS' SAKE *Amen*

AFTER the death of Moses the servant of the Lord, the
Lord said to Joshua the son of Nun, Moses' minister . . .
"As I was with Moses, so I will be with you; I will not fail
you or forsake you. Be strong and of good courage; for
you shall cause this people to inherit the land which I
swore to their fathers to give them. Only be strong and
very courageous, being careful to do according to all the
law which Moses my servant commanded you; turn not
from it to the right hand or to the left, that you may have
good success wherever you go. This book of the law shall
not depart out of your mouth, but you shall meditate on
it day and night, that you may be careful to do according
to all that is written in it; for then you shall make your way
prosperous, and then you shall have good success. Have I
not commanded you? Be strong and of good courage; be
not frightened, neither be dismayed; for the Lord your
God is with you wherever you go." (Joshua 1: 1, 5–9)

For one who has been jilted

O GOD, my world is in ruins about my feet.
I loved him so much
And we were so happy.
But now he has called it all off.

I feel, O Lord, that my heart is broken beyond all
  hope of repair.
I feel, O Lord, that life has really come to an end
  for me.
I sometimes wish that I were dead.
And yet, even in my misery, I remember you.
I remember that you love me with a love that
  never changes.
I remember that you can be trusted never to let
  me down.
And so I catch glimmers of light in the darkness
  around me.
My heart cries in despair that I am beyond help
But my faith protests that somehow you can help.
Please mend my broken heart.
Please start me living again.
Please let me find through time that I can laugh
  once more
And once more look on the world with eager eyes.
FOR JESUS' SAKE *Amen*

COME to me, all who labor and are heavy-laden, and I
will give you rest. Take my yoke upon you, and learn from
me; for I am gentle and lowly in heart, and you will find
rest for your souls. For my yoke is easy, and my burden is
light. (Matthew 11: 28–30)

For one whose keenest hopes have been dashed

O GOD, I am quite sick with disappointment.
I simply do not know how I will get over it—
If I ever do.
I was so set on this.

It meant everything to me.
All my hopes were pinned on it.
But it did not come off and it never can now.
I can scarcely bear the frustration and the an-
guish.
Give me the wisdom to accept the situation.
Give me the courage to face up to it.
Give me the faith to know it need not be the end.
Give me the strength to begin again.
FOR JESUS' SAKE *Amen*

BUT now thus says the Lord, he who created you, O
Jacob, he who formed you, O Israel: "Fear not, for I have
redeemed you; I have called you by name, you are mine.
When you pass through the waters I will be with you; and
through the rivers, they shall not overwhelm you; when
you walk through fire you shall not be burned, and the
flame shall not consume you." (Isaiah 43: 1–2)

*For one who can never have a child of her
own*

O GOD, I would dearly have loved a child of my
own.
This was for so long my hope and ambition,
And now I know that it can never be.
At times I feel quite sick with disappointment and
despair.
And at times I feel very angry toward you.
Help me, O Lord, to believe that you care for me.
Help me to be willing to accept the comfort you
want to give.
And let me come to realize through time
That, though this door must always be shut,

There are other doors which can be opened.
But, Lord, just yet I am terribly hurt and disap-
 pointed.
Please soothe me and heal me and give me peace.
And keep me from being bitter and resentful
Toward other women and their babies.
FOR JESUS' SAKE *Amen*

GOD is our refuge and strength, a very present help in
trouble. Therefore we will not fear though the earth
should change, though the mountains shake in the heart
of the sea; though its waters roar and foam, though the
mountains tremble with its tumult. There is a river whose
streams make glad the city of God, the holy habitation of
the Most High. God is in the midst of her, she shall not be
moved; God will help her right early. The nations rage,
the kingdoms totter; he utters his voice, the earth melts.
The Lord of hosts is with us; the God of Jacob is our
refuge. Come, behold the works of the Lord, how he has
wrought desolations in the earth. He makes wars cease to
the end of the earth; he breaks the bow, and shatters the
spear, he burns the chariots with fire! "Be still, and know
that I am God. I am exalted among the nations, I am
exalted in the earth!" The Lord of hosts is with us; the
God of Jacob is our refuge. (Psalm 46)

For one who is incurably crippled

O GOD, I sigh for the days
When I could move about freely
And which I will never see again.
I hate being crippled like this.
It is not the pain nor the discomfort,

It is my inability to move freely that bothers me
    most.
Keep me, O Lord, from resentment.
Keep me from that bitterness of spirit
Which would act like a cancer on my soul.
And help me to believe, O Lord,
That there may be some compensation to be
    found
Even in such a state as mine.
Let me be willing to look for it
And to accept it if I find it.
There is one thing I want to ask you specially,
    Lord.
Please never let me forget your nearness and your
    love.
For I know that, if only I keep remembering that,
    It will help a lot.
FOR JESUS' SAKE *Amen*

BLESS the Lord, O my soul; and all that is within me,
bless his holy name! Bless the Lord, O my soul, and forget
not all his benefits, who forgives all your iniquity, who
heals all your diseases, who redeems your life from the Pit,
who crowns you with steadfast love and mercy, who sat-
isfies you with good as long as you live so that your youth
is renewed like the eagle's. (Psalm 103: 1–5)

For one who is to have a major operation

O GOD, I am worried and anxious and more than
    a bit afraid.
I keep imagining how things might go wrong.

I keep visualizing disaster and death as the out-
  come.
Help me to be calm.
Help me to have courage.
Let me think of the skill that surrounds me.
Let me have faith in the surgeon who will operate
  on me.
Let me remember that your arms are around me.
May I, then, be unafraid
And may I be serene,
Knowing that the best that can be done for me will
  be done
And that, whatever may come after, I am safe in
  your care.
FOR JESUS' SAKE *Amen*

WHO shall separate us from the love of Christ? Shall tribulation, or distress, or persecution, or famine, or naked-
ness, or peril, or sword? As it is written, "For thy sake we
are being killed all the day long; we are regarded as sheep
to be slaughtered." No, in all these things we are more
than conquerors through him who loved us. For I am sure
that neither death, nor life, nor angels, nor principalities,
nor things present, nor things to come, nor powers, nor
height, nor depth, nor anything else in all creation, will be
able to separate us from the love of God in Christ Jesus
our Lord. (Romans 8: 35–39)

For one who has cancer

O LORD, I can hardly speak for shock and dismay.
I have cancer.
Of course, I have been afraid of this news for
  some time.

I hoped it would turn out otherwise,
But now there is no doubt.
Help me to be calm.
Help me to have hope.
Help me to have faith.
Enable me to cooperate fully with the doctors.
If it is possible, let me make a full recovery.
If this is not possible, let me be courageous and
    serene.
If there is pain, let me bear it with fortitude.
Above all, O Lord, I ask this.
If I am not to get better from my cancer,
Help me to get the better of it through Christ.
FOR JESUS' SAKE *Amen*

THEN one of the elders addressed me, saying, "Who are these, clothed in white robes, and whence have they come?" I said to him, "Sir, you know." And he said to me, "These are they who have come out of the great tribulation; they have washed their robes and made them white in the blood of the Lamb. Therefore are they before the throne of God, and serve him day and night within his temple; and he who sits upon the throne will shelter them with his presence. They shall hunger no more, neither thirst any more; the sun shall not strike them, nor any scorching heat. For the Lamb in the midst of the throne will be their shepherd, and he will guide them to springs of living water; and God will wipe away every tear from their eyes." (Revelation 7: 13–17)

For one whose child has died

O GOD, I am trying not to be bitter or resentful,
But I find it hard.
Please help me.

When I think of this young life with all its prom-
ise,
When I think of its innocence and its laughter,
When I think of the gap it has left,
I feel like screaming, "Why? Oh, Why?"
Keep me mindful of your love.
Keep me mindful of your compassion.
Let me find comfort in the knowledge of your
sympathy,
And that my child is safe in your keeping.
I know that my heartache can not be removed
completely.
I know that my tears cannot be stopped alto-
gether.
But I know that you can help me as no one else
can.
Lord, I believe in you.
Let me believe more.
And give me some peace of mind and heart.
FOR JESUS' SAKE *Amen*

ONE day he got into a boat with his disciples, and he said
to them, "Let us go across to the other side of the lake."
So they set out, and as they sailed he fell asleep. And a
storm of wind came down on the lake, and they were fill-
ing with water, and were in danger. And they went and
woke him, saying, "Master, Master, we are perishing!"
And he awoke and rebuked the wind and the raging
waves; and they ceased, and there was a calm. He said to
them, "Where is your faith?" And they were afraid, and
they marveled, saying to one another, "Who then is this,
that he commands even wind and water, and they obey
him?" (Luke 8: 22–25)

For one who has been bereaved

O GOD OF LOVE, comfort me in my sorrow.
I can hardly believe yet that my loved one is dead,
That I will no longer see him,
That I will no longer hear his voice,
That I will no longer have his companionship.
Remind me that, through Christ, he is not really
    dead,
That he is more alive than ever,
That I *will* see him again,
When I, in my turn, cross the deep river with my
    hand in Christ's.
Even when I remember this, my heart is still sore
Because I know I am going to miss him so much.
Let me come to you with my sorrow,
As a child in tears might come to his father's arms.
Comfort me in my sorrow, O God of Love,
Let me see light through the darkness.
Help me to find peace, though my heart is at
    breaking point.
Make me aware that our separation, though full of
    pain, is a temporary thing.
Comfort me in my sorrow, O God of Love.
FOR JESUS' SAKE *Amen*

BUT we would not have you ignorant, brethren, concerning those who are asleep, that you may not grieve as others do who have no hope. For since we believe that Jesus died and rose again, even so, through Jesus, God will bring with him those who have fallen asleep. (1 Thessalonians 4: 13–14)

For one who faces death at an early age

O GOD, I do not want to die so soon,
But it looks as if I will.
Give me the strength to face it bravely.
Give me the grace to face it without resentment.
Give me the faith to face it without too much sadness.
It has been good to be alive
And I am sorry that my life is to be so short.
But I am grateful for all the happiness I have known.
I am grateful for all my friends and loved ones.
When I am gone, help them not to grieve too sorely.
Help them then and me now to find comfort
In your promise of the life everlasting.
FOR JESUS' SAKE *Amen*

FOR this perishable nature must put on the imperishable, and this mortal nature must put on immortality. When the perishable puts on the imperishable, and the mortal puts on immortality, then shall come to pass the saying that is written: "Death is swallowed up in victory." "O death, where is thy victory? O death, where is thy sting?" The sting of death is sin, and the power of sin is the law. But thanks be to God, who gives us the victory through our Lord Jesus Christ. Therefore, my beloved brethren, be steadfast, immovable, always abounding in the work of the Lord, knowing that in the Lord your labor is not in vain. (1 Corinthians 15: 53–58)

For one who faces death in old age

ETERNAL GOD, I have had a long innings and I
    know it is nearly over now.
Thank you for all the good times I have had.
Thank you, too, for your helping hand in the bad
    times.
Thank you most of all now for the promise of
    another and a better life beyond this.
I have been missing the friends and loved ones
    who have died before me.
I have been losing more and more of them in re-
    cent years.
Before very long I will be meeting them again.
Not that I want to die.
Life is still sweet.
But I do not so much mind dying when I remem-
    ber that Jesus will be with me on the journey.
And when I remember the new life and the re-
    unions it will bring.
Please let me die gracefully and serenely.
FOR JESUS' SAKE *Amen*

"LET not your hearts be troubled; believe in God, believe
also in me. In my Father's house are many rooms; if it
were not so, would I have told you that I go to prepare a
place for you? And when I go and prepare a place for
you, I will come again and will take you to myself, that
where I am you may be also. And you know the way where
I am going." Thomas said to him, "Lord, we do not know
where you are going; how can we know the way?" Jesus
said to him, "I am the way, and the truth, and the life; no
one comes to the Father, but by me . . . Peace I leave with
you; my peace I give to you; not as the world gives do I
give to you. Let not your hearts be troubled, neither let
them be afraid." (John 14: 1–6, 27)

For one who has contracted AIDS

O God, I need your help more that ever
Now that it has been confirmed that I have AIDS.
I was more or less reconciled to the verdict.
All the same it does come as a severe shock to have
    it made definite
And I feel pretty low.
Please help me to be brave
And to make the most of what is left to me.
Help me to use my situation to be of help to oth-
    ers,
Especially those I know who are in the same boat.
And forgive me, please, for every hurt and hin-
    drance
I have caused to fellow-travellers along life's road.
FOR JESUS' SAKE, *Amen*

Blessed be the God and Father of our Lord Jesus Christ!
By his great mercy we have been born anew to a living
hope through the resurrection of Jesus Christ from the
dead, and to an inheritance which is imperishable, un-
defiled, and unfading, kept in heaven for you, who by
God's power are guarded through faith for a salvation
ready to be revealed in the last time. In this you rejoice,
though now for a little while you may have to suffer various trials. (Peter 1:3–6)

For one who contemplates a major disaster

Loving Father, I still address you in this way
Despite this terrible disaster that has occurred
And the tremendous suffering it has caused
But it has taken a conscious effort of will.
So many innocent people have been affected

And it all seems so pointless and unnecessary.
I was tempted for a time, as others sometimes do,
To blame you and hold you responsible
And to rail at you for your cruelty.
But then I remembered how Jesus made it so
    plain
That you love us all at all times and in all circum-
    stances
And even in the worst of disasters, whether per-
    sonal or national or international.
I remembered, too, how you even allowed your
    Son to be crucified
And I realized afresh that you are present in every
    disaster
Loving, sympathizing, sharing, offering strength
    and courage.
Please give them to me now.
FOR JESUS' SAKE. *Amen*

Beloved, let us love one another; for love is of God, and
he who loves is born of God and knows God. He who does
not love does not know God; for God is love. In this the
love of God was made manifest among us, that God sent
his only Son into the world, so that we might live through
him. In this is love, not that we loved God but that he
loved us and sent his Son to be the expiation for our sins.
Beloved, if God so loved us, we also ought to love one
another. (1 John 4:7–11)

For a chronic worrier

DEAR LORD, I have no peace of mind.
I have had none for a long time
And I cannot seem to achieve any.
I worry constantly about everything.
I worry about big problems.

I worry about small problems
And make them seem like big ones.
Help me, Lord, to see things in perspective.
Make and keep me aware that, with Jesus for
    friend,
I really need not worry very much about anything.
For He will always be with me
And, whatever comes, He will keep me safe.
FOR JESUS' SAKE. *Amen*

HE gives power to the faint, and to him who has no might
he increases strength. Even youths shall faint and be
weary, and young men shall fall exhausted; but they who
wait for the Lord shall renew their strength, they shall
mount up with wings like eagles, they shall run and not be
weary, they shall walk and not faint. (Isaiah 40: 29–31)

For one who has been mentally ill

LOVING FATHER, My friends don't really un-
    derstand my illness.
But I know that you do
And that is an enormous help.
Often it is the only thing that keeps me going.
Without that knowledge I think I would just give
    up
When I was having one of my bad spells.
Even then it is sometimes touch and go.
This is such a lonely kind of illness
And I am so much in fear of a relapse.
Help me to live one day at a time
And help me to a feeling of security

Through remembering that your love surrounds
    me always
Irrespective of what I am or what I feel.
FOR JESUS' SAKE *Amen*

HE who dwells in the shelter of the Most High, who
abides in the shadow of the Almighty, will say to the Lord,
"My refuge and my fortress: my God, in whom I trust".

    He will cover you with his pinions, and under his
wings you will find refuge; his faithfulness is a shield and
buckler. (Psalm 91: 1–2, 4)

For one who feels guilty after the death of a loved one

LOVING FATHER, I feel such a weight of guilt.
I keep blaming myself because I think I could
    have done so much better for my loved one.
I keep thinking of the things I did that I should
    not have done.
I keep thinking of the things I should have done
    and failed to do.
The weight of my guilt feeling presses me down
    very hard
And I don't seem able to get rid of it.
I know that you are the only one who can help me.
Please do so.
I am really sorry for any fault that may have been
    mine.
Help me to know that I am forgiven.
Help me to accept that I cannot do anything more
    for my loved one.

Help me to be content that all is well with him
   now.
Please lift my burden from my heart.
FOR JESUS' SAKE *Amen*

HAVE mercy on me, O GOD, according to thy steadfast
love; according to thy abundant mercy blot out my trans-
gressions. Wash me thoroughly from my iniquity, and
cleanse me from my sin! . . . A broken and contrite heart,
O GOD, thou wilt not despise. (Psalm 51: 1–2, 17b)

For one who has been badly let down by a friend

LOVING FATHER, You know how hard I have
   taken it,
How much pain I have felt,
How sick I am at heart.
I trusted him so much
And now I feel so bitter.
Perhaps I have misunderstood what has hap-
   pened.
If so, help me to see the right way of it
If, on the other hand, it is just as I thought it
Please help me to bear it bravely
And to get over it successfully.
However it is, I am grateful that I can depend
   utterly on you,
For I know that you will never let me down.
Help me to find comfort in that knowledge
And may it lead in time to a complete healing of
   the wound I have sustained.
FOR JESUS' SAKE *Amen*

OUR Savior Christ Jesus, who abolished death and brought life and immortality to light through the gospel. For this gospel I was appointed a preacher and apostle and teacher, and therefore I suffer as I do. But I am not ashamed, for I know whom I have believed, and I am sure that he is able to guard until that Day what has been entrusted to me . . . You then, my son, be strong in the grace that is in Christ Jesus, and what you have heard from me before many witnesses entrust to faithful men who will be able to teach others also. Share in suffering as a good soldier of Christ Jesus. (2 Timothy 1: 10–12; 2: 1–3)

For others who suffer

O GOD, I know there are many people in the world
Who are suffering at this moment,
Some of them suffering very badly indeed.
I commend them to your loving care.
Bless the man who is rarely free from pain
And who would give anything for a restful night.
Bless the man whose working days are ended
And who thinks his usefulness is ended, too.
Bless the woman who is going blind
And who wonders how she can ever hope to manage.
Bless the woman who feels very lonely
And who longs desperately for some token of friendship.
Bless the man who has lost a limb
And who doubts if he can ever adjust himself to the new situation.
Bless the woman who has turned quite deaf

And who tends as a result to feel "shut out."
Bless the man who is terrified of falling ill
And who walks an endless tightrope of apprehension.
Bless the woman whose love has been cruelly spurned
And who feels that her heart is broken beyond all chance of repair.
Bless the man whose keenest hopes have been shattered
And who has to live with the knowledge that they cannot be restored.
Bless the woman who will never be able to have a child
And who is bitterly disappointed because of it.
Bless the man who is permanently crippled
And who yearns for the freedom of movement he once had.
Bless the woman who is shortly to have a major operation
And who is afraid of what the outcome may be.
Bless the man who has discovered he has cancer
And who faces the future with a chill at his heart.
Bless the woman who has lost her child
And whose heart bleeds quietly all the time.
Bless the man whose wife has died
And who has found no solace for his sorrow.
Bless those, old and young, who hear death's summons in their ears
And who take wistful farewell of a world they are loath to leave.
Bless, O Lord, all who are in pain or in sorrow or in sickness.

Bless all who are in any affliction of body or of
mind.
Bless all our loved ones, near or far, who are in
special need.
FOR JESUS' SAKE *Amen*

Index

For one who suffers constant pain   85
For one who is no longer able to work   86
For one who is losing his sight   87
For one who is lonely   89
For one who has lost a limb   90
For one who has lost his hearing   91
For one who is afraid of being ill   92
For one who has been jilted   93
For one whose keenest hopes have been dashed   94
For one who can never have a child of her own   95
For one who is incurably crippled   96
For one who is to have a major operation   97
For one who has cancer   98
For one whose child has died   99
For one who has been bereaved   101
For one who faces death at an early age   102
For one who faces death in old age   103
For one who has contracted AIDS   104
For one who contemplates a major disaster   104
For a chronic worrier   105
For one who has been mentally ill   106
For one who feels guilty after the death of a
  loved one   107
For one who has been badly let down by a
  friend   108
For others who suffer   109